How to Raise a Puppy You Can Live With

Third Edition

Clarice Rutherford
David H. Neil, M.R.C.V.S.

Alpine
PUBLICATIONS

P.O. Box 7027, Loveland, Colorado 80537

HOW TO RAISE A PUPPY YOU CAN LIVE WITH:
Third Edition

ISBN 1-57779-022-7

Cataloging-in-Publication Data

Rutherford, Clarice.
    How to raise a puppy you can live with / Clarice Rutherford.
    David H. Neil. — 3rd ed.
        p.   cm.
    Includes bibliographical references.
    ISBN 1-57779-022-7
    1. Puppies —Training. 2. Puppies—Behavior. 3. Puppies.
4. Dogs—Training. 5. Dogs—Behavior. 6. Dogs.   I. Neil, David H.
II. Title.
SF432.R87   1999   99-34985
636.7'0887—dc21   CIP

For the sake of simplicity, the terms "he" and "she" are sometimes used to identify an animal or person. These are used in the generic sense only. No discrimination of any kind is intended toward either sex.

Many manufacturers secure trademark rights for their products. When Alpine Publications is aware of a trademark claim, we identify the product name by using initial capital letters.

Alpine Publications and the authors accept no liability for suggested treatments or training methods mentioned herein. The reader is advised to check with their local, licensed trainer, veterinarian, and other professionals.

First printing of Third Edition 1999
1 2 3 4 5 6 7 8 9 0

Printed in the United States of America.

This book is available at special quantity discounts for breeders and for club promotions, premiums, or educational use. Write for details.

Cover: Head study by Richard Piliero; training photo by Joyce Woolley.
Cover design by Gary Raham
Edited by Dianne Nelson
Text design and layout by Shadow Canyon Graphics

TO ALL THE PUPPY PEOPLE
WHO HAVE MADE A CHOICE

A Contract

I have chosen to share my life with you, a member of another species. I pledge to appreciate your uniqueness as a member of the canine family and to attempt to raise you and discipline you in terms of this uniqueness. In return, I know that you will do your best to fit into my life-style if it is caninely possible and will reciprocate my attentions to you by letting me share your view of the universe. I will also be a better person for having this experience. I hope your life will be better for having been with me.

CONTENTS

INTRODUCTION

*If the status quo prevails, dog ownership is going
to get tougher, and deservedly so . . . . The way we play it
may have very significant impact on the future
of the domestic dog in urban society.*

Every year, countless numbers of people develop relationships with their dogs in work and play, allowing subtle, effective two-way communication to be comfortably established. In some of these relationships, the bond continues to grow stronger, and what begins as a matter of expediency between two awkward strangers — the new owner and the new puppy dog — becomes, in the fullness of time, a meeting of minds and hearts.

At the dawn of civilization in the ancient city of Jericho, there were dogs as large as wolves and as small as terriers. Already man had selected and bred different types of dogs for different functions. This selecting and breeding has continued for thousands of years as a continuous process. Today approximately

200 breeds are recognized by The American Kennel Club, breeds which in one way or another enrich our lives in work and play. We see the amazing adaptation of various breeds to become seeing-eye and hearing-ear dogs. Dogs also assist the physically handicapped. No matter what function dogs perform, the basic underlying theme throughout the vast majority of them is *companionship*. Pet dogs in contemporary society continue to provide a focus of attention and affection for people who feel very much alone, whether confined to their homes or to an institutional setting.

Having praised dogs to the skies, however, we recognize that all is not well with the unwritten contract between man and dog. Too many dogs do not enjoy a healthy family situation and get into so much trouble that they are either impounded or are relinquished to the animal shelter. A high percentage of these animals are approximately eighteen months old and, having outgrown their cuteness, are having behavioral problems that their owners could not deal with. Our purpose in writing this book is to help people understand their puppy's behaviors and needs as he grows into maturity.

We believe that the first step toward getting a dog that you and everyone else can live with — after selecting the right breed for you, of course — is to find a good breeder who recognizes how important the first two months of a puppy's life are in determining how he will be able to deal with the big world as a mature dog. When your carefully selected puppy comes home with you, you are now in the driver's seat, and your knowledge and patient actions will further determine whether you will soon own a dog that you — and your community — can live with.

One of the big issues as we enter the next millennium concerns raising a normal puppy when during the day the entire household is either out to work or at school. We have addressed this issue in the book. Recognizing that separation anxiety is a serious problem, we have addressed this both in terms of proofing the puppy against the development of separation anxiety as well as recognizing some of the signs and dealing with them when they start to occur in later months.

ACKNOWLEDGMENTS

We want to thank Julie Yamane of the Canine Learning Center, and Becky Henson, for access to their puppy classes.

We appreciate the time and effort that Sue Henning has put into evaluating litters in puppy temperament testing, and her work on the evaluation form.

CHAPTER 1

CHOOSING YOUR PUPPY

The best puppy for you is the one that will grow up into the right dog for you. When choosing a puppy, you must be able to visualize what the adult dog will be like physically and behaviorally.

When you visit a litter of little puppies that are so easy to handle and control, it is easy to overlook the thought that within a few months these puppies will have the size and general behavioral characteristics of their breed, together with the individual behavioral tendencies inherited from the parents. Unfortunately, when you select one of them and take him home, you might be unhappy with the result, because that little puppy can change into a much larger and more vigorous dog than your home and life-style can manage. It isn't the pup's fault that you didn't give some thought to the adult dog that the puppy would become.

1

The best puppy for you is the one you can live with, and everyone else can, too. When choosing a puppy, you must be able to visualize what the adult dog will be like physically and behaviorally, and how he will fit into your home facilities as well as into your life. For instance, a person who would be very content with a relatively slow-moving Basset would probably be frustrated with a quick-moving, high-energy terrier.

Perhaps the first deliberate action in acquiring a puppy is to set aside sufficient time to familiarize yourself with all that the world of dogs can offer you, and, in turn, what you can offer a dog. During this time, you can resort to the abundant literature on dogs and seek expert advice. In this way, you start to zero in on that special little chap that will so enrich your life in the future.

A puppy's adult personality will be shaped by a combination of three factors — his breed, his individual genetic behavior, and the socialization that he receives during the first four months of life. Breed characteristics are generalizations, of course, but they are recognizable in most members of each particular breed. It is obvious that different breeds not only look different, but behave differently. Don't pick a breed on its looks alone — you could be surprised.

Breed Characteristics

When you begin reading about the different breeds, note the history of each one. This informs you of the specific reasons for which they were bred and the purpose they served for their humans and gives you an idea of the built-in behavior and attitude of those breeds.

Dogs are descended from the wolf, whom we know to be a hunter, a herder (to direct his prey in a particular direction), a guard (to protect his food supply and his den of cubs), a team player (to work together to run down prey), an athlete (that can lope across many miles), and an aware animal (that has intensely acute senses of sight, scenting, and hearing). Each of these qualities is called a "drive."

The different breeds were selected to emphasize one or more of these drives, which then became part of the dog's personality. For example, the Collie, the Shetland Sheepdog, and the Corgi were bred for herding sheep and cattle, and you might find yours herding a group of children in your yard by circling around them. The northern breeds, such as Siberian Huskies and Malamutes, were selected in their gene pool for pulling and going forward continuously. Your Husky will need to be on a leash or he might decide to take off on a run. The purpose of the sporting breeds is to find game, with the retrievers specializing in returning the game to their person. You will find them picking up and carrying things around the house. The scent hounds have an intense scenting ability, and when they catch an interesting scent, they follow it regardless of what you say. But they still bond to their person. This is the basic difference between dogs and wolves.

The terriers, which were bred to hunt and catch small animals, are quick moving with high energy and are always ready for a chase. Working dogs such as German Shepherds and Rottweilers know that they have a job to do for their humans. They were expected to protect flocks from wolves, coyotes, and mountain lions, as well as to protect their humans. Toy breeds were bred to be companion dogs that prefer spending time close to their humans.

When you select your own puppy, think about the characteristics that were bred into that particular breed, which of the drives are strongest, and what that tells you about the future behavior of your dog. Try to be objective when you decide whether those characteristics will fit with your own personality. Think about the dog's need for exercise, his activity level in the house, his attitude toward visitors, and his trainability.

Once you have decided on your breed, you will find a range of personalities within that breed — some more quiet, others more dominant. Look for the pup that fits the image you have for your canine companion.

A good source of information about the breed in which you're interested is your local kennel club, which can give you the names of breeders. Many of these clubs periodically run an ad in the pet section of the local newspaper. When buying a puppy, you're not just buying a pedigree — you're buying the expertise, the understanding of the puppy's needs, and the advice that the breeder can give you based on experience with that particular breed.

Another source of information is to attend a dog show and buy a catalog of the dogs entered. This lists the names and addresses of the people who are showing, and you can follow up by contacting a breeder in your area. *Dog World Magazine,* found at many magazine stands, and the *AKC Gazette,* found in many libraries, list breeders in all parts of the country.

When you contact a breeder, you will probably be asked questions about your life-style and about the plans that you have for your dog. Do you have enough time to give your dog? Good breeders want to be sure that the puppy goes to a good home.

We cannot recommend buying puppies that are born in puppy mills (and usually sold in pet stores). You cannot learn anything about the parents of the puppy and will know nothing about the treatment that the puppy received during the sensitive stages of birth to eight weeks, nor about hidden health problems.

Notice the mother dog's attitude. Is she friendly to you? In this photo the pups are weaned. *Photo by James Digby.*

When you have selected the breed that has a size and disposition best for you, it is time to consider the individual personality that you want your pup to have. A good indication of this is the personality of the parent dogs. Behavior is a hereditary factor, just as are the appearance, the length of coat, or the type of head, and behavior is of greater importance to most buyers. Therefore, if either parent is very shy or very aggressive, you will want to look at other litters before making a choice. Conversely, if the parent dogs like people and are pleasant to be around, you will know that there is a good chance that the pups will have the same qualities. The puppy will not be a carbon copy of either parent but will likely have some of the behavioral characteristics of each.

The third aspect of a puppy's personality is the socializing that he receives from the breeder and the behavior molding that he receives from his new master. Every breeder knows that careful breeding is only part of the story, although a very important part. Breeders have seen a promising puppy ruined by bad training or simply a lack of training, or by mismatching a puppy with a certain type of person. If a breeder tells you that he doesn't think a dog is right for you, he does so from experience based on placing puppies.

Choosing Your Own Puppy

Selecting a puppy is often a matter of deciding which pup most likely fits your personality. For example, if at seven and eight weeks of age a Labrador Retriever puppy is running around as fast as he can, grabbing your pant leg, crashing into you when you're down on your knees, jumping up into your face, or grabbing at your hand when you try to pet him, then you can be certain this puppy will be a handful. Another Labrador puppy in that same litter may be quiet, may come to you slowly at first, and may lick your hand or face. This pup will be much easier to train, and because he's a Labrador, you know he will become sufficiently lively when he is acquainted with his new home. Which pup is best for you? Perhaps you prefer a pup that isn't always fussing for attention. An independent pup that is busy sniffing, not caring whether he's petted, might develop into the type of dog you would want once you have bonded to each other.

Many breeders have puppies that are reserved ahead of time, so each person gets a pick. For example, you might have the third-pick female because two people reserved a pup before you did. Another person might have fourth-pick male (if there are that many). It might seem that you won't get the pup that's best for you, but the breeder often helps match puppies and people, and it's amazing how the pups seem to go to the most suitable homes. Many breeders use puppy testing and their own evaluation to match puppies and people. You can also use your own guidelines. See the Appendix on Puppy Temperament Testing.

When you visit a litter, observe the cleanliness of the puppy area. Ask if the puppies are socialized by family activities. *Photo by James Digby.*

Observation of a pup with his littermates sometimes gives a false impression of the pup's innate desire to please and to adjust to people. Never select a puppy based on his behavior with his littermates. Remove him from the litter and play with him individually. Observations made by an inexperienced buyer on only one visit may not accurately reflect the true puppy — the hellraiser might be tired, and the wallflower may have just awakened and may be feeling his oats. More than one observation, the breeder's opinions, and testing will give a better rounded picture and may prevent a mismatch.

If you have the pick between two or three puppies, carry one puppy away from the litter, far enough so that the pup can't see or hear his littermates. Is the pup curious, wagging his tail, and exploring? Is he worried and trying to return to the litter? Can you attract his attention by clapping your hands, or by bending down close to him and having him run to you? Does he follow you when you walk past and coax him? Does the pup look at you when you hold him close and talk to him? Roll the pup on his back and hold him gently. Read the score sheet in the Appendix to evaluate his reaction. The final decision on your part might be an emotional one, but part of that selection process is based on how you react to the puppy on a one-to-one basis. The puppy that you *don't* want is the shy pup that wants to run and hide or the aggressive puppy that nips at you when you try to play with him.

When You Can't Visit the Litter

You will have to trust the breeder if you can't visit the litter. Ask all the questions you can think of. Tell the breeder the type of puppy you want, then rely on the breeder to make the final decision. Many breeders require a deposit if you want a puppy held for you. The remaining payment is made when you pick up the puppy, or just before shipping. You should receive the puppy litter registration at this time or a written promise that it soon will be in the mail.

The Best Age to Acquire a Puppy

Many breeders have considered seven weeks to be the ideal age for a puppy to leave his littermates and go to his new home — never younger. Others prefer to keep their puppies in the litter until ten weeks of age. Some states now have a law that prohibits selling a puppy before eight weeks of age. There is a federal regulation that a puppy can't be shipped by air before eight weeks of age. Because of the eight-week fear period, it is best to wait until nine or ten weeks of age. It is advisable for the buyer to be guided by the experience of the breeder. The main concern for the new owner is to be certain that the pup has received sufficient individual attention and puppy training from the breeder.

The Older Puppy

If you are considering a puppy that is twelve weeks or older, you need to get two assurances from the breeder. First, the puppy must have been taken out of his pen on a regular basis to experience different environments; otherwise, kennel shyness may develop. Second, the puppy must have spent time alone with a person on a regular basis (for example, fifteen minutes a day, four or five days a week); if not, his socialization will be retarded, and much time and effort will be necessary to bring the pup to a normal attitude toward people and other dogs. If these two aspects have been taken care of by the breeder — in other words, if the puppy training has begun — you can do just fine by buying an older puppy.

Don't Take Home Two

If you want two puppies, wait until the first pup is five to six months old before bringing home the second. By this time, the pup will have bonded to you and will be comfortable spending more time alone in his yard or house area. The problem with

Puppies learn bite inhibition from each other. If one bites too hard, he suffers the consequences. Puppies should not leave their littermates before seven or eight weeks of age. *Photo by James Digby.*

littermates is that the initial bonding is to each other rather than to you. If they have each other, neither pup will give you his full attention. This makes training almost impossible. Modern research in dog behavior indicates that puppy-human bonding is essential to a superior relationship. It's a very rare person who can induce bonding with more than one puppy at a time.

Other Considerations

Unfortunately, some individuals raise puppies only for what financial gain they might experience, and they care nothing about the needs of the puppies. Don't hesitate to ask for specific information. Get a detailed report of what care and activities have been done with the puppies, and find out how knowledgeable the person is about the characteristics and history of the breed. If the breeder seems lacking in any of these areas, don't fall victim to a hard sell. These people should not be encouraged to perpetuate their puppy activities. They do more harm than good for the dog world.

There are many conscientious and reliable breeders who breed and raise puppies with great care. Take the time to find the right one. A good breeder will tell you why he did *this* breeding and will share with you his expectations for the litter.

We have the advantage of raising and training dogs in a time when much has been discovered about the basic developmental periods of a puppy's life. This is very exciting. We can take what heredity gives us and then control the environment to develop the best possible personality in the adult dog.

Dogs must pant
to keep cool.
*Photo by
Anita Stewart.*

CHAPTER 2

BEHAVIOR:
THE ENVIRONMENTAL FACTOR

*Urban living does not come naturally to a dog, but by
understanding a puppy's needs, we can help him to adjust.*

A major portion of this book pertains to the first six months of
a puppy's life with emphasis on the first three months. There's a
good reason for this. We believe that these early months are absolutely the key to molding a dog's behavior so that he can fit into
the complexities of life in the twentieth century. Let's face it, urban
life isn't exactly a natural environment for man's best friend —
but with care it can be one to which he can adapt.

Life was great for the dog in small-town America where the
family dog went everywhere with the kids and also had his own
circle of friends among the other dogs in the neighborhood. In

contrast, most dogs today live isolated lives in backyards, pens, or homes, completely at the mercy of a few members of the family who are often very busy with other activities. If the dog is fed every day and has shelter, we are too likely to think that we're filling his needs.

The dog is by nature a pack animal with definite social needs. Through the millenia while man and dog were evolving, the dog developed empathy with humans and a desire for attention from his human pack members. If this need for attention is ignored the dog can become very frustrated and might well begin to indulge in activities like incessant barking and destroying property. If the dog is not only kept in such an environment as an adult, but is bred and raised with inadequate attention, the problem is compounded.

Dog behavior studies have determined that the first twelve weeks of a dog's life are vitally important because a puppy's experiences during this time will affect his emotional responses as an adult dog. It stands to reason, then, that if we know how the puppy is growing and what the puppy needs during these different stages, we can help every puppy get the best possible start in life.

The need for human attention begins shortly after the puppy is born. During the first few weeks of life the pup is going through the most amazing process of growth. At first, his world is dark and silent and consists solely of contact with his littermates and the constant care of his mother. After about two weeks he begins to learn new behaviors which will adapt him well to living in a sensory and social world. By eight weeks of age he has full use of his sensory and motor systems and his central nervous system has reached maturity, ready for whatever learning experiences await.

The puppy's central nervous system, and therefore his behavior, develops in a wondrously particular and precise pattern, and each stage of growth has an effect on the puppy's actions. If the pup doesn't have his physical and social needs satisfied during any one of these periods, certain characteristics of his personality will be stalled at that particular stage of development. This, in turn, will have an effect on how the dog will behave when he is older.

For example, some dogs remain overly suspicious of anything new or different, often because they never developed investigative behavior when it was a normal part of their growing up (eight to

Photo by Deloris Reinke.

twelve weeks). Another dog might be too easily excited, to the extent of appearing hyperactive, as a result of not having had adequate environmental stimulation during the stage of learning how to sort out sounds, sights, and smells (six to ten weeks). And both the shy and the hyperactive personality can be strongly affected by a lack of human contact from three to seven weeks.

You are undoubtedly wondering if knowing about these developmental stages in a puppy's life is all that important. Obviously, many dog owners have raised very fine dogs without such information — for good reasons. These pups may have had outgoing personalities and have been able to overcome some lack of socialization. Even more likely, these pups were fortunate enough to be raised in homes where their needs were automatically and unknowingly met during each period. Dogs have been successfully socialized for more than 10,000 years without anyone being specifically aware of it, let alone labeling the process!

So it is today in many homes. Puppies that get a lot of attention and receive touch, sound, and visual stimulation in the course of a normal day grow up to be healthy, well-adjusted dogs.

But not all puppies are so carefully raised. If the breeder is away from home during the day, for instance, a certain amount of time must be reserved in the evening for puppy activities. This is why timing the arrival of a litter is important. A concerned breeder checks the calendar when planning a breeding to make sure that puppies will not be neglected. If certain social obligations or an unusually heavy work load will occur at a certain time of the year, a litter should not be bred to arrive at such a time.

The breeder who is not willing to give some time to the puppies should let someone else do the breeding and puppy raising. There are enough poorly adjusted dogs in the world now that did not get the people-care they needed while they were puppies.

This is where the so-called "puppy mills" are totally negligent. The people who operate these mills have a large number of female dogs whose only function is to produce puppies for profit and who are often kept isolated in cages, boxes, or other very small areas. This so-called "breeder" has no understanding of the needs of the dog and does not realize the damage done to a pup's personality by giving it no socialization during the first eight weeks. It is not only extreme cruelty to keep the parent dogs in such confining isolation, but it is also cruel to the puppies to deny them the socialization they must have if they are to adjust to living with people as they grow up.

Today, so much has been learned about dog behavior that there is no excuse for a socially maladjusted dog. Whether you are a breeder who is introducing the world of dogs to newcomers, or whether you are a first-time puppy owner, there is much you can do to make this a good world for your pet. You don't have the luxury of many days and weeks to be a partner in your puppy's personality development. But you don't have to give up a normal routine and become a "puppy-recluse" in order to accomplish your goal. Mostly, you just need to be aware of what's going on in the natural process as a newborn puppy grows from a "blob" into a bouncing young adult.

CHAPTER 3

THE DEVELOPMENTAL PERIOD
(The First Three Months)

*Experiences during the first three months are the
foundation of the puppy's mature personality.*

The first three months of a dog's life are called the developmental
months because it is during this time that almost all of the dog's
basic behavioral patterns are developed. At least the first seven
weeks of the puppy's life are the responsibility of the breeder.
Beyond that age, the responsibility for socialization shifts to the
new owner. Each period has specific activities that can help a
puppy grow emotionally.

There are three basic developmental periods in the first twelve
weeks. These periods are defined here by calendar time, but this
doesn't mean that all puppies will begin each period on exactly

the same day. There will be variances depending upon the breed and upon individual differences within the litter. Littermates usually catch up with each other, however, by the end of the last period.

Table 1. Basic Developmental Periods

Neonatal Period	Transitional Period	Socialization
1-14 days	15-21 days	22-84 days
birth to 2 weeks	2 to 3 weeks	3-12 weeks

In order for us to understand a puppy's needs as he begins to grow, we should become familiar with the characteristics of the different periods. This chapter will cover the general description of each period. Chapter 4 will discuss the breeder's role in raising puppies, and Chapters 5 and 6 will deal with the new owner's activities in taking a puppy to his new home.

The Neonatal Period

1-14 days	**Key Puppy Behavior:**
	Spends about 90 percent of time sleeping
	Susceptible to excess heat or cold
	Crawls
	Nurses
	Seeks warmth of littermates and mother
	Can usually right himself if turned over
	Needs anal stimulation for urination and defecation

At this stage the bitch is the main influence on the puppy. Her health, milk supply, and attitude toward the pups, and later toward people who come to look at the puppies, will influence the behavioral development of the litter. If she is overly fearful or aggres-

Photo © Clifford Oliver.

sive, this can be imprinted on the puppies and their future behavior might be very similar to hers, whether or not they were born with a fearful or aggressive genetic trait. Thus, a behavior can be either genetically or environmentally derived.

At this age, the pup's abilities are confined to sucking, vocalizing, and crawling slowly. The senses of sight and hearing are not functional yet. The eyes may begin to open around ten days of age but in most cases are not open until about fourteen days of age.

The puppy learns about his environment through touch. You can observe him crawling around, moving his head from side to side until he bumps into his mother or a littermate. A puppy might crawl away from the bitch, but she should be able to retrieve him by carrying him in her mouth, providing he doesn't crawl out of her sight or sound. Urination and defecation are reflex responses that occur only when the bitch licks her puppies' anal and genital region.

During this period, the pup is aware only of heat, cold, and pain. He is not yet capable of regulating body heat efficiently and therefore needs his mother and the other puppies to help maintain his own warmth. Even though it looks as though the pups do nothing but eat and sleep, this is a very important period. The central nervous system is rapidly developing, getting ready for the next stage.

The Transitional Period

15-21 days	Key Puppy Behavior:
	Eyes open
	Teeth begin to emerge
	Gets up on four legs and takes a few steps
	Begins to lap liquids
	Defecates without the mother's stimulation

The puppy's eyesight is dim, but he is ready for the next adventure. He discovers that the other pups are more than just warm lumps to be crawled over and slept on. He begins to stagger around on four legs, lifting himself up first on his front legs, then on the hind legs as they become equally strong. Activity periods are brief, followed by sleep to gather strength for the next concentrated effort. By the end of this transitional period, the pup can walk on four legs and lap milk or soft food in a fairly efficient manner (although not very elegantly).

The pup no longer needs constant care from the bitch and is beginning to defecate without her stimulus. He starts to get interested in littermates. The very beginnings of pack-oriented behavior, such as pawing at each others' faces and chewing on littermates' ears, are seen at this stage.

The Socialization Period

Socialization is the name given to the next nine weeks, the growth period lasting from three to twelve weeks of age. We have found that this period can be divided into four stages, each of which is an important stepping-stone for the one that follows.

Photo by Judith Strom.

The dog's primary social relationships develop during this time. If his primary relationships are with people, the pup will be able to form lasting relationships throughout his life, but the puppy that receives little human contact during this time will find it difficult to adjust to humans as long as he lives.

The puppy also needs to be with littermates and the bitch during the first weeks of the socialization period. He needs to learn how to act around other members of his own species, or he could become a dog that picks fights easily or has problems with mating (if this should subsequently be desired).

The Period of Becoming Aware
(First Stage of Socialization)

22-28 days	Key Puppy Behavior:
3-4 weeks	Can hear, see, and the sense of smell is becoming much more complex
	Begins to eat food
	Begins to bark, wag tail, and bite other pups
4-5 weeks	Uses legs quite well but tires easily
	Paws
	Bares teeth
	Growls
	Chases
	Plays prey-killing games

We have divided the socialization period into four stages not only for ease of discussion but also because the behavioral patterns of the puppy are readily distinguishable and determined by their physical age. The central nervous system continues to develop rapidly during this time. The puppy now has both sight and hearing ability and by four weeks is beginning to develop perception of distance. The sense of smell, which is one of the first to develop, is now starting to develop a subtlety that becomes such an important part of the perception of the world by the adult dog.

The beginning of the socialization period can be determined for each puppy by using the startle-reaction test. *When a puppy visibly reacts to a loud sound, he is into the socialization stage.* This is also a means of telling which pups are on a slightly different time schedule in their physical development. This is valuable information because otherwise these pups might unjustly be labeled as dull-witted or slow when actually the only problem is that they need time to catch up physically with the others. Puppies, however,

Puppy begins to show
interest in food.
Photo by Deloris Reinke.

don't always go by the book and react on the twenty-first or twenty-second day. One breeder accidentally dropped a pan about four feet from the puppies on the eighteenth day and got a big reaction. On the twenty-first day the puppies didn't react to a loud noise. By then they apparently accepted it as part of their world.

Even if we didn't look at the calendar or use the startle test, we would know when this period begins. It's as if someone pushed the "on" button. Virtually overnight, the puppy turns into an animated little being.

From twenty-two to twenty-eight days, the puppy is experiencing a shower of sensory stimulation. So much awareness of the world around him is happening so suddenly that the pup needs a very stable home environment to balance the excess stimulation. The bitch should remain with the litter as much as possible during this week.

By the end of the third week, the pup displays much more complex behavior than at the beginning of the period, which is an indication of how rapidly development occurs. The pups now play

During this period the bitch can be separated from her puppies occasionally during the day, but her presence is still important to the puppies. *Photo by Deloris Reinke.*

together. They start to learn how much chewing and biting the other pups will take. They begin to show adult behavior patterns with their play-fighting, scruff-holding, and prey-killing (head-shaking) movements, and they are beginning to bark, growl, and snap at each other. Some pups begin barking and wagging tails around three weeks of age, but this varies with the breed and the individuals.

It is possible for many a puppy's behavioral patterns to get stalled at this stage because he isn't allowed to act normally during the next two periods. This occurs especially among the toy breeds because of attitudes toward their size, but it can happen with any breed. When a puppy is not ever allowed to act like a dog (i.e., rough-and-tumble playing with other pups, investigating all corners of his world), never experiences stress of any kind, and has all his needs met before they even arise, he becomes a spoiled pet — a perpetual puppy. The breeder is cheating the dog by not allowing him to develop into a mature canid, and the owner is cheating himself of the pleasure of having a mature dog as a companion.

The Period of Curiosity (Second Stage of Socialization)

36-49 days	Key Puppy Behavior:
5-7 weeks	Weaning begins
	Curious
	Little sense of fear
	Participates in group activities and sexual play
	Dominance order is beginning

This is an *extremely important* time in the puppy's life. It is the period when the pup is totally dependent on the environment that you provide for him to stimulate and develop his genetic qualities. In addition to needing a stimulating environment, the pup must receive attention from people. The kinds of experiences that a puppy has during this period have a very strong effect on how he will react emotionally to humans when he is an adult. If he has little contact with people, except for being fed, he's probably not going to find it easy to accept human attention when he's older.

This is another time of rapid growth and change. During this period, a puppy acquires full use of his eyes and ears, his legs become stronger and more coordinated, and his brain reaches a final stage of physical development. Further development now largely depends on the experiences encountered by the otherwise fully equipped puppy.

At the beginning of this period, the puppy still has little sense of fear and is quick to approach anything and anybody. But by the end of these two weeks, he begins to be more cautious in his approach, which is all a part of learning to discriminate among sights, sounds, and smells. Pups that don't go through these two

The center puppy is demonstrating a dominance posture.
Photo by Janet Yosay.

periods of learning (having been isolated or overprotected) tend to become hyperactive adults. They have not learned how to sort out sights, sounds, and smells during these weeks and to identify the significant ones.

Sexual play is evident at this age. Mounting is quite common among male puppies, and sometimes females mount other puppies. This is a normal part of puppy play and is important in teaching puppies what is normal sexual response as they mature. While mature males tend generally to confine their mounting to females, mounting to signify dominance over another male continues in maturity. Females also sometimes mount other females as a demonstration of dominance.

Many behaviorists agree that socialization reaches a peak by the forty-ninth day. From here on, human relationships, though still very important, begin to have a decreasing effect on the socialization of the puppy. In other words, the amount of individual attention that a puppy has received by the forty-ninth day can never be made up without a proportionately larger expenditure of time and effort.

The seventh week (forty-ninth day) is considered by many breeders to be the right age for a puppy to go to his new home. By then the pup has had sufficient time with his littermates for developing adequate dog behavioral patterns. His new owner can easily become the pack leader and can give the pup individual attention and a lot of environmental variety. It is still essential, however, that opportunities for socializing with other dogs be made available on a regular basis. This ensures that the balance is maintained in interactions with other people and with dogs in the community.

The Period of Behavioral Refinement (Third Stage of Socialization)

50-63 days 7-9 weeks	Key Puppy Behavior 7 weeks: Has total hearing and visual capacity Will investigate anything 8 weeks: Fearful of sudden and loud sounds and movement Cautious of anything new in the environment

The period of behavioral refinement is characterized by progression from unfettered curiosity to a more nervous evaluation of the stimulus created by the pup's environment. This reaches its height around eight weeks of age and persists to about ten weeks of age.

This stage is an important milestone in a puppy's life. He reaches full visual and hearing capacity, and his brain is physically mature. This means that the brain is ready to perform its physical processes and the pup can start learning to respond to your wishes as long as the learning process is taking place in very small steps. However, this doesn't mean that he's ready to be treated as an adult dog. He is still emotionally very immature.

This age is sometimes termed the "fear period" because the pup is very susceptible to long-lasting effects if he receives a bad fright during this time. Dr. Michael Fox has observed that at five and six weeks, a puppy can be severely frightened and in a relatively short period of time bounce back to his normal happy self again. However, during the eighth week, if the pup receives a bad fright, it may take weeks for him to return to his normal behavior in the same frightening situation. He may even carry the fear all his life. A loud, rough person, a spanking, or an abnormally sharp noise are examples of frights that can cause such a reaction. Thus, shipping a puppy to a new home by air freight during the eighth week could have a lasting bad effect. But don't think that you have to go to the other extreme and be overly protective, keeping your pup in seclusion. Let him have normal experiences.

Puppies at this age also become hesitant about new and different objects and situations. During the preceding period (five to seven weeks), the puppy usually approached the unfamiliar fearlessly. Now, at eight weeks, the pup is noticeably more hesitant in his approach. He may go back again and again to the same area or object as though he doesn't trust his initial judgment.

An example of this caution is seen with retrievers — the five- to seven-week-old puppy will splash in shallow water or happily bounce into heavy grass, cattails, or whatever is in his path. But during his eighth week, this same pup will start to be suspicious of water, even a shallow pond, or a pile of rocks, and he seems to think that diving into a patch of weeds is unthinkable, at least without a lot of sniffing and investigating first. However, by the end of the ninth week, this very pup is returning to his previous crash-bang self.

This is all another normal and important part of the socializing process, a continuation of sorting out the multitude of smells, sounds, and sights to determine what is important.

The Period of Environmental Awareness (Fourth Stage of Socialization)

64-84 days	Key Puppy Behavior:
9-12 weeks	Develops strong dominant and subordinate behavior among littermates
	Begins to learn right behavior for right time
	Continues to improve in motor skills
	Has very short attention span

Even though no new behavioral patterns are evident during these weeks, the pup is beginning to learn the right behaviors for the right times. This is no small task, and it is a necessary stage for the pup to go through in the maturing process. His brain is ready for full functioning, but information must be fed into it one step at a time. It takes a puppy a long time to learn the acceptable ways of the world. This age is the culmination of the socialization process. Exposure to different environments (as discussed in Chapter 6) is the primary consideration here.

Up to this age, the puppy has been very self-oriented. Most of his learning has been "me"-directed. He has learned to like his new family. He knows where his bed is, where the food is kept, where there's a warm place for a nap, and (very importantly) where the urinating and defecating areas are. Now he's beginning to pay attention to *you*.

In fact, he thinks you're wonderful! He'll quickly learn his name. He'll come flying to you when you call him and get his attention. At this age, the puppy has a strong desire to please. After all, you're his whole world, having taken the place of mother and littermates.

The puppy pays attention to you, but he's also extremely busy learning everything he can about the world around him. The pup's brain tissue reached its full physiological growth around eight weeks of age, and now he's ready to learn, to have experiences that will teach him how to behave, how to act like a dog, how to

Developmental Periods of the First Three Months.

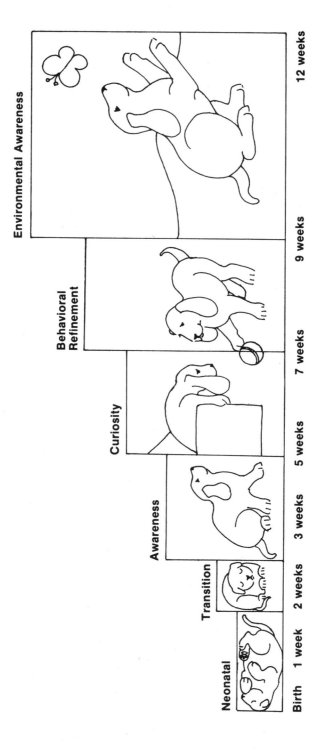

Neonatal	Transition	Awareness	Curiosity	Behavioral Refinement	Environmental Awareness

Birth   1 week   2 weeks   3 weeks   5 weeks   7 weeks   9 weeks   12 weeks

Table 3. Summary of Puppy Behavior—What You Can Expect

1 and 2 weeks	All activities are innate—only sucking, crying, crawling and touching. No sense of sight or sound. Is susceptible to cold temperatures. Must receive touching from bitch to stimulate elimination. Cannot learn anything at this age.
3 weeks	Eyesight and hearing dim but rapidly improving. Begins to walk briefly. Becomes interested in littermates. Able to start eating and drinking and to eliminate without the bitch's stimulus.
4 weeks	Needs a very stable environment. Becomes aware of multitude of sights and sounds. Learns that people are important. Should remain with bitch as much as possible.
5 weeks	Life becomes exciting! Not afraid of anything. Is very aware of people and likes to be with them.
6 weeks	Has full use of eyes and ears. Legs stronger and more coordinated. Investigates everything in sight.
7 weeks	Very involved with his own needs. Will seldom respond to name. (You must take initiative if you want him to follow you.) Can be started on housebreaking routine.
8 weeks	Occasionally responds to name. Hesitant about approaching new things. Needs to be able to take his own time about new experiences.
9 weeks	Will follow at your side for short distances. Likes to lie down beside or on top of your feet.
10–12 weeks	Almost always responds to name and comes when called from short distance. Will come running when he hears food pan rattle. Learns not to get stepped on. Becomes more dependable with housebreaking.

Photo by Margie Thayer.

please a human — quite a challenge for a pup, but one that he's ready for.

By ten weeks of age, strong dominant and subordinate behavior is displayed among littermates. In some cases, this behavior has been evident for three to four weeks. Any puppies remaining from the litter should start receiving individual attention and should receive their own special time alone with the breeder or other individual. Otherwise, the pups will begin bonding with each other, will lose their interest in people, and will become more difficult to train.

The last stage of socialization is a most delightful one. At the same time that you should be actively molding your puppy's behavior (he won't always be this small and eager to please), you should also be enjoying your puppy. Relax and have fun. A puppy stays little such a short time — he'll be grown up before you know it.

Photo © Click the Photo Connection.

This ideal bitch is calm and relaxed with her puppies.
Photo by Kent Dannen.

CHAPTER 4

THE BREEDER'S RESPONSIBILITY

*A puppy's most important behavioral needs during his
first seven weeks are exposure to mild stress,
a stimulating environment, and individual attention.*

Being a breeder of puppies is an important job — one that should be undertaken with a commitment for the time and effort necessary to get the pups off to the best possible start. Aside from a clean, warm box area and good diet, a young puppy has definite behavioral needs. The breeder is the person who supplies these needs. During the first seven weeks, a puppy's three most important needs are exposure to mild stress, a stimulating environment, and individual attention.

Exposure to Mild Stress

Even though the bitch is the primary influence in the puppy's life for the first twenty-one days, the breeder can at this time begin to influence a puppy's future behavior. Although the pup's eyes don't open until the end of the second week and his hearing isn't functioning until the third week, he will respond on a purely physical level to being touched. Touching and lifting the pup begins to condition his physiology to react, at a very low level, to changes in his experience.

The First Two Weeks

Breeders who have made a practice of handling pups at a very young age have observed that these pups become very outgoing and confident as they get older. A study by Dr. Michael Fox

During their first two weeks, puppies can benefit from brief, mild stimulation. *Photo by James Digby.*

verifies and expands this observation. After conducting a study on the heart rates of puppies, he concluded that mildly stressing puppies will develop dogs that are superior when put in learning or competitive situations. Puppies that are handled at an early age and exposed to mild stress on a physiological level are better able to handle stress later in their lives without becoming emotionally disturbed or indulging in hyperactive behavior. As a result, they learn quickly and are more responsive to new experiences in different environments.

Dr. Carmen Battaglia, in his article "Developing High Achievers," tells of a method developed by the U.S. military to improve the performance of dogs used for military service. It is termed the BioSensor Method, known to the public as the Super Dog Program. Based on research, the military studies confirmed that there are specific periods of time when neurological stimulation

Puppies need daily attention, and it is important that they receive it. *Photo by James Digby.*

has important effects. The first period is a window of time between three days and sixteen days during which there is rapid neurological development. Simple exercises at this time affect the neurological system by pushing it into action earlier than would happen normally, resulting in an increased capacity for future learning. Benefits include improved cardiovascular performance, greater resistance to stress, and greater resistance to disease.

You can simulate these exercises with your own puppies. Pick up each puppy every day. Rub his softness against your cheek, and admire his miniature perfection — these are the fringe benefits. Hold him for about a minute, with the puppy's body firmly supported by your hand under his tummy. Weigh him if you desire. Using both hands, hold the puppy in an upright position, then in a head-down position, and finally on his back, cradled in your hand. Touch a foot.

Don't pick up the puppies any more during the day, unless necessary, of course. Children should not hold puppies at this age. Too much stress has a negative effect on the puppies' development.

Weeks Three to Seven

During these weeks, the activities involve the senses and are stressful in the sense that these are new stimulations to the puppies. In the third week, pick the puppy up and use your thumb and finger to put light pressure on the ear or the foot. If he squeaks, he should calm quickly. For these pups, repeat by touching, with no pressure at all, and progress to a slight pressure the next day.

The fourth week, twenty-two to twenty-eight days, is a very stimulating one for the puppy. He is aware of the many sights and sounds around him and is quite excitable. About midway during the week, take the pup away from his littermates and put him on a different floor surface than he has experienced before. As well as being a stress activity for the puppy, this is also valuable for observation of the pup's behavior and doesn't take more than three to four minutes per puppy.

Put the puppy down on cement, wood, dirt, or fine gravel, or linoleum if it isn't too slick for walking. If the area is bare, place a jacket on the floor, or place a chair or anything that represents a different object for the pup to either approach or ignore. After

One-on-one time with the puppy can include teaching the stand for a few seconds. *Photo by James Digby.*

you have put the pup down on the floor, begin to record how he reacts to being alone, how quickly he begins to cry, whether he walks around or stays in one place, or if he investigates with his tail wagging.

You can already begin to see differences in personality in the litter, and it is interesting to keep a record of these. Make a note of which pups are the most aggressive feeders and which ones lose out in competition and always seem to end up on the outside of the puppy pile. Which pups are the noisiest? Which ones squirm and cry when picked up, and which ones settle down and enjoy it?

The most extreme behaviors stand out first, of course, but don't forget to notice the pups that are in the middle range of temperament. These are the pups that likely will be easily trained as they grow older. Infrequently, it can happen that a pup will show signs of brain damage, such as being able to move only in a tight circle. If you observe unusual behavior, consult your veterinarian about the severity of your particular case.

If the litter is large and the same color, a dot of fingernail polish in different areas on the puppies or a collar of different-colored rickrack tape helps identify them as individuals.

During the fifth and sixth weeks, give the pups mild auditory and visual stress. On one day during each week, play a radio for a few minutes near the puppies when the pups are awake. Play it at a loud but not blaring level. If you have normal hearing and it sounds loud but not irritating to you, it will be sufficient. On another day, give the puppies mild visual stress by flicking the room lights (not in bright daylight) for two or three minutes.

By the fifth week, individual attention by the breeder will become one of the mild stress activities because a small level of stress exists each time the puppy is removed from his littermates and taken to a different area where you are the main focus of his attention. Many pups show no evidence of stress; others will be hesitant but will become more confident with each experience.

Individual Attention

The interaction of the puppies with the bitch and with littermates is profoundly important for at least the first five weeks. If you want a puppy that is well adjusted to his identity as a canid, then his relationships with other dogs are very important. For example, the puppy learns from his littermates and his mother just how much of a bite is too much. He learns through this experience that he must control the use of his jaws.

As the pup approaches the age of five weeks, the period of curiosity, he begins to explore and will leave his mother and his littermates at times. Among wild canids, other adult members of the pack would interact with the pup, but with the domestic dog, this is the point at which people begin to take over the role of the canine mother, virtually reliving history and in so doing reinforcing the domestication of the puppy into the human world.

At five and six weeks, friends can help with socializing.
Photo by James Digby.

Time spent alone with each puppy helps him learn that the name of the game is to be with people and to pay attention to people. Personal attention helps the puppy develop a feeling of his importance as an individual. This, in turn, helps him grow into a happy dog eager to please his owner. One-on-one time with a puppy opens the second window of limited opportunity — socialization. This period of time is between the fourth and sixteenth weeks of age. Lack of socialization during these weeks inhibits social and psychological development.

By the fifth week, twenty-nine to thirty-five days, the central nervous system has developed substantially, and the puppies now have sight, hearing, and smell (or scent) and are beginning to develop distance perception. However, even though the pups need the stimulation of people, sights, and sounds, emotionally they are still very immature and they tire easily; therefore, a little attention goes a long way. At least once during this week, but preferably twice, each puppy should be taken away from the

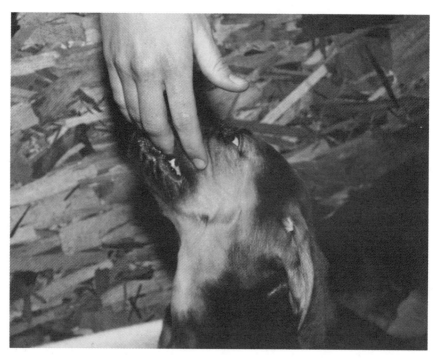

Learning bite inhibition on people begins with this puppy at six weeks. *Photo by James Digby.*

puppy-pen area for at least five minutes. The time can be spent with informal play. Bend down so that your face is close to him, allowing you to interact on your puppy's level. Eye contact and facial expression offer a more intimate interaction.

This is a good age for new people and children to play with the puppies, provided caution is taken to see that the pups aren't overstimulated. In fact, if there are no children in the home, invite children to visit the puppies.

During the sixth week, thirty-six to forty-two days, it would be very unfortunate if the breeder neglected to see that each pup got individual attention. People who visit the puppies can help. In the fifth week, the pup probably wasn't too interested in a person, but now, at six weeks, most pups will run toward a person and try to climb into a lap or jump on legs. A two-way communication system is developing.

During the session, call the puppy to you from three to five feet (on your knees and patting the floor or ground). Walk closely in front of him, and coax him to follow by patting your leg. Sit down on his level for some gentle play. Stroke the pup. Talk to the pup; with your voice, try to get him to look at you.

Occasionally, there's a puppy in a litter that acts shy and is uncomfortable when taken to a different room or area. He may not want to come to you or may not even want to walk around and investigate the area by himself. When working with this puppy during his individual session, be sure that you are where the pup can neither see nor hear his littermates. Sit down on the floor or ground near him. Don't lean over him — that will only make him more fearful. Talk to him in a quiet voice. Pat your hand on the floor in front of him. Try to get his attention. See if you can coax him to come to you even if it's just a matter of his moving a few inches. This pup needs much gentleness. If you're an impatient person, don't try anything that will make you irritated if the pup doesn't respond the way you think he should. Just spend the time sitting close to the puppy. If neither of you moves for the first session or two, that's the way it is. The puppy will gradually become accustomed to your presence and will begin to approach you and investigate. He should be placed with a person or a family who understands that this puppy will require special attention to develop into a socially functioning puppy, and that he will always remain very sensitive to his environment.

Environmental Enrichment

Beginning with the third week, the puppy is busy learning to use his rapidly developing senses. We know from behavioral and physiological studies how rapidly the pup's nervous system is growing during the next several weeks. At this age, brain cells are growing, and if they aren't stimulated, they won't develop into the pathways that give the pup his best learning potential.

You don't need to dazzle the puppies with a clutter of items. Do your pups play in the backyard? Lawn furniture is an example of environmental stimulation. Moving the wheelbarrow

Toys strung across the puppy box add special interest and can be changed weekly.
Photo by James Digby.

Introduce the four-week-old puppy to a new walking surface.
Photo by James Digby.

This bottle contains items that rattle when bumped. In the background is a cardboard box for getting into or chewing.
Photo by James Digby.

around for cleanup is another example. This is what we mean when we say that a litter raised in a family home environment is automatically socialized and stimulated. However, when pups are raised in a pen or kennel, specific items need to be added.

Use whatever is available to you. For example, set a couple of old wood stumps in the pen area. Cardboard boxes are marvelous and fall in the easy-come, easy-go category. These can be dens for a pup to go into or tunnels to walk through. One item that's very popular with one breeder's pups is a wood box about four feet long and two feet wide, open on the ends, with carpet. The pup can go in one door and out the other or lie inside and look out, or run through, or whatever seems right at the time. Another idea is short lengths of plastic or ceramic pipe — whichever size your pups can easily walk through. (Never take a chance with a pipe that might become too narrow as the puppies grow.)

Toys

The first concern in selecting toys is safety; obviously, toys should not be breakable or sharp. A wide range of chewing and play toys is available in pet-supply stores, but a puppy isn't interested in how much money you spend. For a young pup, a good toy is something he can pick up in his mouth or push and roll with his nose. A small plastic bottle with a pebble in it for noise is great fun for a puppy. For safe chew toys, a pet-supply store is the best source. (All puppies need chew toys for their human's sake!)

Puppies have preferences, and what attracts one may not interest another. A toy has no value if it's too large, and it's dangerous if it is too small. A sturdy glove is a good toy; for example, a worn-out leather glove is ideal. Think of the wealth of odors it has! A couple of knotted socks of different textures can be a lot of fun for pups who like to shake a toy. Rotate the toys so that a different selection can be available every few days.

The Breeder's Role

Not all puppies are fortunate enough to start their lives with caring and informed breeders. But those who do have an invaluable head start. We appreciate the fact that a large number of breeders in all breeds in all parts of the country look at this labor as one of love.

Principle Guidelines for Breeders

1. Plan a litter when you are able to provide the time and facilities necessary for proper socialization and care.
2. Select breeding stock with sound, well-adjusted personalities from a line of dogs with good temperament.
3. Temperament test the litter at seven weeks of age.
4. Cull from your breeding program any dogs that produce poor temperament such as shyness, aggression, or nervousness in their puppies. Also cull any dogs that exhibit bad behavioral traits that puppies may learn from association, such as barking and growling at people.
5. Spend at least five minutes every other day handling each puppy during the critical stage of five to seven weeks.
6. Provide stimulating facilities and toys for the litter. Introduce each puppy to a variety of environments before he leaves for his new home.
7. If you place a puppy in the eighth week, be certain that the new owners know about the fear period. Any loud sound or sudden movement can create a fear that will take much time and effort to overcome.
8. Educate your puppy buyers in the proper socialization, training, and handling of the puppy, and try to assure yourself that the buyer is interested enough to put in the time for this training and socialization before you sign the sales contract.
9. Follow up with your puppy buyers, and help them resolve behavioral problems at the onset.
10. Maintain contact with puppy buyers to determine how the pups mature into adult dogs. Correlate this information with your notes on individual puppy temperaments. With experience, you will refine your ability to predict temperaments.

CHAPTER 5

PUPPY GOES TO A NEW HOME

"Enjoy getting acquainted with your dog, but don't expect too much too soon."

Nothing equals the excitement of anticipating a new puppy! The fun of bringing a pup home and introducing him to his new family is a very special experience. What hopes we have for our perfect puppy! He will, of course, become a well-mannered dog, staying quietly at our side, eager to follow our every command. Well, it's a long road from the cuddly puppy to the mature dog, but with some effort and understanding, it can be traveled successfully. It all begins with Day One in the new home.

The first few days a puppy is in his new home can be trying for both the puppy and the new owner, because both are trying to adjust to a new situation. After all, the puppy finds that he has been suddenly taken from his den and littermates and is expected to immediately accept a new, foreign way of life. However, with patience and a sense of humor on the part of the new owner, the first few days can be accomplished with good feelings on both sides.

Breeders and behaviorists generally agree that seven weeks of age (forty-nine days) is the ideal age for a puppy to go to his new home, with seven to ten weeks being the most desirable age range. In families where there are preschoolers, we recommend that a pup not be introduced into the home during the eighth week.

The seven- to ten-week-old puppy still needs a lot of rest and will take morning and afternoon naps. For the first day or two, however, he might be very excited and spend much of the day in motion, checking out his new home. As long as he isn't hurting himself or anything else in the environment, let him investigate wherever and whatever takes his fancy.

Children should not be allowed to overtire the puppy.
Photo by Jan Whitaker.

If the puppy is eight weeks old when he first comes home, be very patient with him. This is the fear period, and sharp noises or harsh treatment will leave him with fear that may take months to overcome. Let him take his time getting acquainted with everything, and don't take him to places where he will be subjected to loud and frightening sounds or activities. If at all possible, trips to the veterinarian should be arranged either before or after the eighth week.

If the puppy is ten to twelve weeks old when you first bring him home, he'll be more rambunctious, especially if he's one of the larger breeds, and he'll sleep considerably less during the day. However, he's at an age where you can get his attention quite easily and where he'll want to please you and stay close to you. It's very important that the puppy's pre-training activities begin now.

The First Day

Before the puppy arrives at your home, we assume that you will have made adequate preparations, such as a bed with a blanket or a piece of carpet in it (a cardboard box works fine for this). Know where the puppy will be kept when you're absent from home during the day (backyard, kennel, or a puppy-proof room), know where you want the puppy to urinate and defecate, and have a supply of puppy food on hand and a food bowl and a water bowl. You will be much more relaxed if you have thought out these details before the puppy arrives.

The main concern with the first few days is in letting the pup get acquainted. Within the area where he is allowed to roam, give him lots of time on his own to sniff and explore, to find his bed area, to determine good nap-taking spots, and to learn where his food and water dishes are kept. Feed him a good-quality puppy food; the breeder of the pup will inform you what the puppy is currently eating. The seven- to eight-week-old pup is probably eating four times a day, which can be changed to three times a day, and around four to six months of age, to twice a day. We prefer scheduled mealtimes to free feeding because it helps with house-training. In addition, it shows your pup how reliable you are in the food department — same place, same time, same good food every day. As your pup grows, he'll gradually need to increase the amount of food, but don't let him turn into a butterball. Sometimes, because of an owner's work schedule, free feeding is the better solution. In this case, the main concern is that the pup doesn't overeat. Measure the amount of food put in the feed dish to keep a record of the quantity being eaten.

If the puppy is going to be kept in a pen area for a certain amount of time each day, be certain that he has a few toys available, and be certain that he won't be left for long periods of time. The ideal situation is for a puppy to be with someone a good bit of the time for the first week or two. The best time to initiate a puppy into your life, especially if the family is working or in school most of the day, is to arrange for the puppy's arrival during a period when someone will be home on vacation, at least for the first several days of the puppy's arrival.

The most difficult part of the puppy's first day is the first night in a new and strange place. This subject deserves a section of its own.

First Night Alone

The puppy's first night alone in his new home can be one of intense fear. The fear of suddenly being left alone can lead to anxiety that can show up later as a behavioral problem, such as excessive barking or digging at the carpet.

There aren't many alternatives for a pup's first night, and it is certain to be a stressful experience to some degree, but there is one method that works very well. Let the puppy spend his first couple of nights in the bedroom of his new master. Put a box in the room with a blanket or carpet in it, or just put the bedding on the floor beside your bed. The pup might ignore your efforts and select his own place, like under the bed or in a corner. Let the pup stay wherever he will relax and settle down.

A puppy is usually exhausted by nighttime and will sleep through the night. If not, a hand reaching down in the dark helps to calm him. (If this doesn't work, you'd better get up and take the pup out to urinate.) First thing in the morning, carry the pup outdoors

Keeping the puppy in the bedroom the first two nights makes the adjustment to a new home much easier for both the pup and the people.

or to the area covered with newspapers. You usually will have to carry him, because he might not be able to walk as far as that by himself without urinating until he's ten to twelve weeks old.

Two nights, or sometimes three, is usually enough of this special treatment. By then the pup should be ready to accept his bed in the regular place that you have selected for him. If you don't plan to allow the pup to continue sleeping in your room, it's best not to let him stay past the third night. If you wait much past that time, the pup will reach a point where he won't want to be moved, and you'll be back to where you started with the crying. If these special measures aren't possible, you had better buy some ear plugs and be prepared for loud crying for at least two nights.

You may want to consider allowing the puppy to continue sleeping in the bedroom. If you work and are away from home a lot, this is one way of giving your dog a sense of your presence and of your desire to be with him as much as possible.

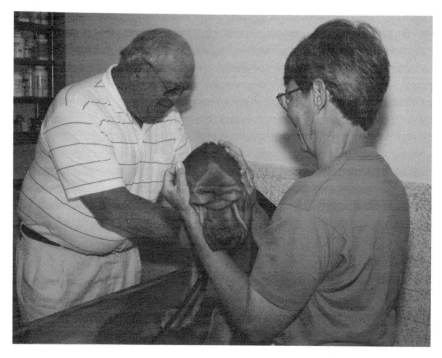

Your veterinarian can answer any questions you might have.
Photo by James Digby.

If you decide to do this, you should keep the pup in a crate during the night, or put the pup on a short rope tied to a leg of the bed until he's house-trained, with his own bedding there also, of course. The rope should be short enough to allow him to lie down without getting tangled.

Your Veterinarian

Your veterinarian is a vital member of the puppy-raising team. We believe that it makes good sense to select your veterinarian, and preferably get acquainted, before you even select the right puppy for you. Veterinarians deal with many breeds of dogs in sickness and in health and are only too happy to counsel you during that important time when you are making decisions about dog ownership and familiarizing yourself with the do's and don'ts.

Your veterinarian, if consulted early in your puppy's life, will be able to advise you of the things that you should be looking for and will make arrangements in advance for complete health counseling, checkups, and vaccinations.

If you have already acquired a puppy and have not yet consulted with a veterinarian, put this book down and do so right now. The veterinarian may not want you to go down there immediately, but he or she will make sure that a plan for a healthy and happy future for your puppy is worked out with you and subsequently implemented.

House-Training

Have you ever put a puppy outdoors, left him there for fifteen to twenty minutes, then let him in again only to have him immediately make a puddle or a pile on the carpet? It's very easy to believe that he's doing this on purpose, and it's very easy to get very angry. However, the pup simply doesn't have it all figured out yet. For one reason or another, he's still confused about the indoor-outdoor situation. Besides that, he doesn't urinate and defecate until he has the urge, and he didn't happen to get the urge until he was in on the carpet. It's going to take some time on your part to help him get the whole procedure straightened out. Some puppies learn in a few days, some not until they're three and four months old. Some puppies simply don't have the muscular control until they're several months old.

People tend to get very excited over the process of house-training. What's needed is a realistic philosophy — plus a lot of paper towels and carpet deodorant.

At what age can you expect your pup to be reliable in the house? The answer is as variable as the puppies to whom it applies. In puppy classes, we have owners who say that their pup had only two accidents and has been trained ever since. Other owners say that their pup is four months old and sometimes still has an accident. Some pups adapt to a routine very quickly, and some people adapt to being consistent in training. Some pups have stronger muscle and bladder control than others. There are many factors that affect the age at which your pup will be reliably trained.

As explained in the discipline section, spanking does more harm than good, and this is especially true in house-training. Many puppies react negatively to spanking. This can create additional problems and often actually prolong the training procedure. The least painful approach for both the owner and the pup is to establish a routine and to praise the puppy for performance at the proper time in the proper place. Follow these guidelines:

- Feed the pup at the same times every day, and when he's finished eating, immediately take him outdoors. Take the puppy out immediately after he awakens from a nap and after a play period, or even in the middle of a play period if it's a long and vigorous one.
- Keep your pup in the same room with you where you can watch him. If necessary, tether him to you by tying a long line around your waist so that the pup can't get more than three or four feet away from you.
- When you can't keep an eye on him in the house, put him outdoors or keep him in his crate — not longer than two hours for eight- to ten-week-old puppies, and not longer than three to four hours for older pups. Every time he comes out of his crate, take him outdoors immediately.
- If you are gone during the day and the pup is kept in the house, confine him to a room that's easy to clean and that can be mostly covered with newspapers (or you can simply clean up the floor). Gradually decrease the space covered by paper to only one small area. When the pup is older, probably around three months of age, remove the paper and train him for outdoors only.
- Take the puppy to the same outdoor area each time, and stand around and wait. If he doesn't do anything, return to the house, leaving him outdoors for a while if possible. Watch him, then go out and praise him if he does anything. If he comes in without

doing his chores, take him back out every five or ten minutes until he has success.

- If you catch your pup in the act, don't spank, but tell him what you think and rush him outdoors.
- Clean up and deodorize the area with either a vinegar-water solution (one part vinegar to four parts water) or a commercial cleaner. Otherwise, when a puppy gets a whiff of that particular odor, an eliminative reflex is set off, and thereafter he does what is natural for him.
- For nighttime, remove the water dish a couple of hours before bedtime. Take him outdoors at bedtime, then put him either in a small, easily cleaned room or in his crate at your bedside. A pup can sleep several hours in a crate, and he will awaken you when he needs to go outdoors. Most pups adjust to their owners' sleep schedule reasonably quickly, depending on the age of the pup.
- Praise your pup every time he does his chores in an appropriate place. Praise shows the puppy what you want him to do and where.
- Use a key phrase, such as "hurry up." This will help in the future to cue your dog to get busy and stop daydreaming.

For the pup that is still not house-broken by four to four and a half months of age, get busy with your puppy training. Evaluate the relationship between you and your pup. Are you alpha? Does the pup respond to you when he hears his name? Does he come to you when you call from a short distance? Maybe your pup thinks that the house is his and that he can do whatever, wherever he wishes.

House-training is your responsibility. The pup is only doing what comes naturally.

Crates and Kennels

Another means of controlling the puppy so that he doesn't have accidents when you're not home is to train him to stay in a crate. As with everything else in puppy training, this is done gradually.

Giving your pup a treat gives him a positive attitude about going into his crate. *Photo by Beth Baily.*

Have the crate always available, leaving the door open. Drop pieces of his food inside, and he'll quickly become very comfortable with going in to eat the pieces. Use it as his bed if possible. You can feed him in it. When you first close the door, stay there with him, talking to him. Open it after a few minutes and praise him, even if he did make a fuss. It will gradually become his "place" and he'll feel very secure in it.

The puppy shouldn't be confined continuously (except at night), but a crate can be a big help for an hour or two at a time. As the pup grows older, he can spend longer periods of time in a crate as long as it isn't a regular long-term arrangement. A crate is also excellent for car travel. It keeps the dog safe from sudden stops and swerves, and it keeps the people safe from an excitable dog.

There's nothing cruel about using a crate. It's very natural for a dog, because it fits into his den concept. Most dogs that have their own crates consider them a place of security. The only conceivable problems arise if the pup is forced into the cage suddenly and becomes frightened, or if he is left in it for hours at a time and becomes excessively lonely and bored.

Some families find a backyard kennel or pen area a necessity for confining the dog to a particular area of the yard. This offers protection for flowers and landscaping during the puppy's rambunctious growing-up months or when the puppy is left outdoors with no people present. These can be made of chain link and can be an attractive area, easy to keep clean.

Care must be taken, however, not to put the puppy in his kennel and then forget about him. Everyone in the twentieth century is busy, but if you're too busy to have the puppy out of the kennel everyday to be with you in the house or in the yard, then you're too busy to have a dog. Yard kennels are a convenience if used properly but should never be considered for twenty-four-hour-a-day confinement.

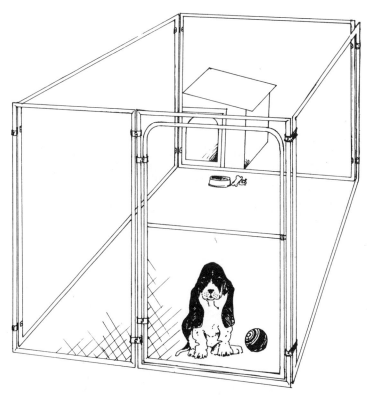

A pen keeps the pup from destroying plants in the yard but the puppy should be trained and played with every day.

Play

Play is an important part of the maturation process. A puppy learns what his abilities are by playing — play sharpens the senses of sight and scent. Play also stimulates the brain, keeping the pup alert and interested in his environment.

Play can be as simple as a running game — inviting the pup by giving the canine signal for play (a play-bow, putting your hands on your knees and bending over). Take a quick step, and the pup will probably start running around you in a circle. After the pup learns his name, you can play hide-and-seek — hide when you call him to come to you. Run up the stairs or to the next room, or behind a door. Keep calling until he finds you and discovers how happy you are to see him. Another running game is the round-robin. Position family members or friends around the yard. Take turns calling the pup, and have each person praise the puppy enthusiastically before the next person calls.

Puppies can make a game out of an old rag. *Photo by Deloris Reinke.*

Balls are great toys
and provide oppor-
tunities for interac-
tion with your pup.
*Photo by Joyce
Woolley.*

A variety of toys encourages play, and a toy box on the floor for storage keeps them from cluttering the house. A squeaky toy and a puppy is a delightful combination, with the pup pouncing, tossing, stalking, and seeing how much noise he can produce. Soft, stuffed toys made for dogs are marvelous fun, but if your pup will rip it apart, it can't be left in the toy box — just get it out for short periods of time when you can watch. Put a knotted sock in the toy box for this pup. One pup had a teddy bear for his favorite toy, and he never chewed it — he just carried it around — and it was still a favorite two years later. This, however, is an exception. Balls are great toys. To begin, just sit on the floor with your legs out and roll the ball. When your pup has it, pat the floor to

When you see your pup in action, praise him and give him a treat. *Photo by James Digby.*

encourage the pup to run back to you. With the older pup, bounce the ball and have the pup learn to catch it in the air. Balls designed to roll in crazy directions are a delight for many puppies. Retrieving is a good game for exercising your pup.

Chew toys serve multiple purposes — pups love something hard to vent their chewing desire, and this also starts to wear off the sharpest points of their baby teeth. Sterilized bones, nyla bones, and rawhide pieces serve this purpose. Use rawhide sparingly if your pup tears it apart too quickly and swallows the pieces. Shoes, socks, magazines, purses, baseballs, and mitts are also some of a pup's most favorite toys. If you don't want your puppy chewing these items, however, keep them out of reach.

Play hide-and-seek with your pup's toys. Put a toy behind a piece of furniture. "Where's the squeaky? Find it!" Help him to find it until he learns the game. Use the name of his favorite toys often. Pretty soon, he'll learn which toy to go get from his toy box when you call it by name.

Tug toys are a very popular item in pet stores and can be used either to good advantage or, with some pups, not used at all. For independent pups that don't have much interest in playing with you, a tug-of-war game allows you and your pup to interact with each other and to develop your own version of the game. For other pups, tug-of-war games encourage aggressiveness or excessive mouthiness. These pups obviously shouldn't play this type of game. A rule of thumb to determine how much of this characteristic is in your puppy is to note his tendency to get too excited and your inability to halt the game. If the pup won't stop, tears your shirt sleeve, grabs at your hand, and loses control of his bite inhibition, this game isn't for him.

Most puppies will readily play with other dogs and puppies, as well as by themselves with a favorite toy, but the play that we truly want to encourage is a one-on-one activity. It's worth the effort, because there's nothing sadder than a grown dog that doesn't know how to have fun with his people.

Puppies and Older Dogs

Young puppies should never be left alone with older dogs unless you *know* beyond a doubt how the older dog treats rambunctious youngsters. There's a good reason for this. Some puppies don't begin to show submissiveness until they're about four months of age. Until they reach that point, they don't have an ounce of sense around older dogs and will usually pester them until the dog puts a stop to it. This might be done in a manner that doesn't injure a dog, such as scruff-shaking or snapping and growling. However, it might also be done with a bite that can injure a small puppy seriously. Don't take that chance.

By the time the puppy is four months old, the risk of injury becomes much less. The pup begins to assume the submissive posture of rolling on his side when threatened by an older dog, and this acts as a damper on the situation. A puppy at least four months old knows enough to move out of the way quickly, too.

Photo by Judith Strom.

CHAPTER 6

SOCIALIZATION CONTINUES
(Eight to Sixteen Weeks of Age)

*The growth of the dog's brain is complete in half a year
compared to eighteen years in humans. Think about that
and about how fast these first puppy weeks fly by.*

Prepare Your Puppy for the Future

With the information gathered from brain research in recent years, we are beginning to understand the whys of working with our pups at an early age. "The more sensory stimulation that the dog's brain receives," states Bruce Fogle, DVM, in *The Dog's Mind,* "the more developed his mind will become." Sensory and physical activities cause nerve cells (neurons) in the brain to grow and make new synaptic connections with other nerve cells. This results in a network that expands to accommodate and assimilate new information.

61

Experiences during the pup's first months determine the actual wiring of the brain. Each time your pup learns a new activity, makes eye contact, responds to your voice, plays with you and others (including dogs), he stimulates the connections in the networks of the brain. These connections, called synapses, are strengthened when stimulated and become part of the brain's permanent structures. If the synapses receive no signals from the neurons, they wither away.

How Do You Deal with the Neuron Responsibility?

Take a leave of absence from your job? Spend at least twelve hours a day with your pup? Smother him with structured activities? No, that's not necessary. But plan to give your puppy as large a variety of experiences as you can during these early months. If you work, your pup should be top priority when you're home.

Stimulate Those Neurons

Physical activities introduce a variety of challenges that stimulate the growth of brain cells. Help your pup navigate the rungs of a ladder lying on the ground and walk a board about twenty-four inches wide, two feet off the ground. Teach him to climb an A-frame (or any inclined surface that has cleats), run through a tunnel (available in toy stores, or use a long box with the ends removed), and climb up and down wide stairs. Other activities include jumping over fallen branches or a broomstick set six to eight inches off the ground. Don't try to show off and have your pup jump higher. The same goes for taking your pup jogging with you. At this age, the pup should have short walks. The joints shouldn't be stressed. Check with your veterinarian.

The pups in the photos are three to four months old and are in an indoor puppy class. If puppy classes in your town are outdoors and, because of the vaccination schedule, you want to wait until your puppy is four months of age, devise these exercises at home. Use your imagination. You don't need specially constructed items. Introduce these activities at as young an age as possible.

Mental exercises stimulate the growth of brain cells and the connecting synapses. Teach your pup to catch a treat. Practice makes perfect. Later, add catching a bouncing ball. Teach him the names of his toys by repeating the name when you play with

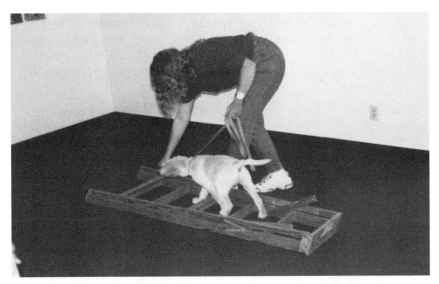

New experiences for your puppy can be found around the house.
Photo by Author.

him. One day he'll surprise you by bringing the toy you ask for. Hide a dog biscuit in the room for your pup to find by sniffing. Let him watch you, then help by guiding him close to it. After he knows the game, teach him to find a favorite toy.

The best part about having fun with your puppy is that he uses his senses — looking, listening, scenting, touching, and tasting (a variety of tidbits keeps his interest high). His agility increases with all of the different movements and with the muscle and mental activity.

Eye Contact

You want your pup to look at you when he hears his name. (Don't overdo this. A hundred times a day is *not* good.) At ten and twelve weeks, the pup wants to look at you because you are his world. Take advantage of this. Each time he responds to his name and makes eye contact, reward him with "good dog" or a command such as "come" or "sit" when he knows them. Sometimes, as a reward, clap your hands or scratch behind his ears — anything that's fun.

An eight-week-old Daschund puppy learns to give eye contact for a treat.

Some pups, especially independent, shy, and very active puppies, need your feedback even if they only begin to turn their head in your direction. The more hesitant, distracted, or busy your pup is, the more you need to work on the timing of your praise the instant he looks toward you. Teach your family about this. Children are notorious for nagging a dog by repeating his name. Then, when the pup does look, the kids are distracted, forgot what they were doing, and ignore the dog. Adults have this problem, too. A friend complained that her four-month-old puppy never paid any attention to her. While we visited at the park, I watched her call his name three times within twenty seconds. He glanced at her two times, but she never said "good" or smiled or in any way acknowledged his glance. The third time, of course, he didn't bother looking. You should expect your pup to pay attention to you. But first you must concentrate on what *you* are doing and pay attention to your pup.

If you have other dogs living at home, make the effort to spend time with the puppy one-on-one. Take your pup with you whenever you can to buy dog food at a feed store or to visit a friend. Take him for walks. If you know of a field or area that has ups and downs, rocks, fallen trees, and limbs — that's ideal. And, of course, use some of your time together just having fun.

Socialization

It's easy for us to get preachy about this because it's so vitally important. It's difficult for you, the puppy owner, to know what the fuss is all about because you don't see any specific results from your socialization activities. And you probably can't recognize the behaviors at one to two years of age that are symptoms of a lack of socialization or indicators of success, because you will naturally assume that your dog's behavior has nothing to do with his activities when he was two to four months of age (and seven to nine months of age, which is a secondary socialization period).

Here are the facts. The undersocialized dog often becomes fearful of anything new — people, dogs, places, anything. This is shown by excessive barking, anxiety, dog aggression, fear, and

Buy your puppy food at a pet-supply store and socialize your puppy, too.
Photo by Author.

hyperactivity. The socialized dog is confident around people and other dogs and seldom displays anxiety in new environments. Best of all, he will calm down after a vigorous play period rather than stay wound up. Socialization introduces more learning experiences. The undersocialized dog has a brain that lacks the huge array of neural connections of the well-socialized dog that lives in an enriched environment with toys and home activities.

How do you socialize your pup? Quite easily. If it's available for you where you live, a puppy kindergarten class brings together new puppies and new people in a new environment. You get a lot for your tuition fee. Choose places that are safe to take your puppy, because you probably haven't finished your puppy-shot series yet. This includes visiting neighbors, friends, and out-door areas that you know aren't frequented by dogs running at large. Some pet-supply stores welcome their customers' dogs.

Think about the potential places and people in your town and about your life-style. There might be more possibilities for social-ization than you realize. If you're gone during the day, leave the radio or TV on and have toys that can be stuffed with biscuits or cheese. Change toys daily. A rawhide chewy might ease the stress of departure time for both of you.

Socializing your puppy isn't complicated, nor does it involve anything that is not a part of your life or your family's life. But please remember — there is so much to do, and such a short time in which to do it.

Introduce the Puppy to Pretraining Activities

Building self-confidence and teaching a pup to do different things is a round-robin situation. The more confidence a puppy has, the better he learns. By the same token, when a puppy is learning to do new things, he is also gaining more confidence in himself and in his abilities.

This type of puppy activity is not a rigid training session. We're working with emotionally immature animals that are sus-ceptible to fears and to confidence-destroying tactics similar to those that affect the human child. The term "pretraining" better indicates the intent of these activities, assuming that such a term does not belittle their importance. We assure you, work at this age will pay big dividends in the learning attitude of your dog when he is older.

The Collar

Puppies should become comfortable wearing a buckle collar at eight weeks of age. Continually check the collar for tightness, because pups often grow in spurts and a collar can become too tight in a very short time. Do not use choke-chain collars with puppies.

The Leash

Puppies need to learn about leashes, which should be as light-weight as possible. Thick leashes, whether they are made of leather or cotton webbing, are too stiff and heavy. A lightweight leash will be usable long after your pup grows up. Chain leashes aren't acceptable.

Leash Training

Clip the leash to the collar, and when the puppy starts walking, go his way. Follow for a minute or two, then release the pup from the leash. Another suggestion: Some pups get very excitable on the leash, so when the pup is in the yard and ready to go back into the house, put the leash on him when he's trotting happily. He'll be intent on returning to his home area and shouldn't be bothered by the leash. Then there's the pup that insists on chewing the leash. Encourage him to pay attention to you by coaxing with your voice and patting your leg as you walk. Keep the puppy moving at a brisk pace — almost a run — to keep his attention on you. If he insists on tugging the leash, spray some Bitter Apple, available at pet-supply stores, on the part the pup usually grabs.

The Sit

Pups are never too young to begin doing sits. Anytime you have a couple of minutes and the pup is there with you, do two or three sits in succession. You don't need a leash on the pup for

Good hand position for teaching the sit. The leash is used for training in the park but isn't needed in the house. *Photos by Jane Exon.*

this. One method is the jackknife procedure. One hand will be on the pup's chest, the other under his tail behind his knees. Say "sit" while you jackknife the pup into a sitting position. To do this, push back on his chest and forward on the rear of the stifle joint (behind the knees). The puppy is wiggling, so practice your coordination and do it quickly. Praise him immediately. Don't make the puppy stay in a sitting position — that comes later.

The other method of teaching the sit is discussed in the training chapter. Hold a tidbit right on top of the pup's nose, and move it back parallel to the floor. The pup will sit as his head moves back to follow the tidbit. Praise him as soon as he sits.

The Come

Begin teaching the come from seven weeks onward. Teach it anytime and anyplace around the house or yard. You do not need to have a leash on your puppy for this. The young pup loves to come running and lick you in the face. You are his whole world. Take advantage of this, expecially with the shy and the independent puppy that might initially resist coming to you. Get the pup excited while you are standing right in front of him, then run backward several feet. Give lots of happy praise and a tidbit — even independent pups usually can't resist a piece of hot dog, cheese, or cooked liver. If your pup is busy and easily distracted, begin the come at very short distances — maybe three to

Begin teaching the come as close as necessary to get the pup's attention. *Photo by Joyce Woolley.*

four feet. Begin as close as necessary to get the pup's attention and to achieve success. Gradually lengthen the distance. What's important at this stage is the pup's attitude — he *wants* to come running to you because it's such fun.

Grooming

Brushing should be included in the puppy's routine by this time. Begin very gradually. Thirty seconds is long enough to have the puppy standing (relatively still) while you brush him. Praise him when you are able to accomplish a couple of brushes. This is important, because the puppy must know when he has pleased you. Gradually increase the length of time you work with the pup. You'll notice a slow, steady improvement in his cooperation. If you've timed your praise well, the pup will realize that grooming is a pleasant experience to be shared with you even though tangles might occasionally complicate the situation. While you work with your puppy, tell him how handsome he is

Teaching the young puppy to stand will help with combing and brushing.

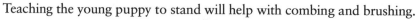

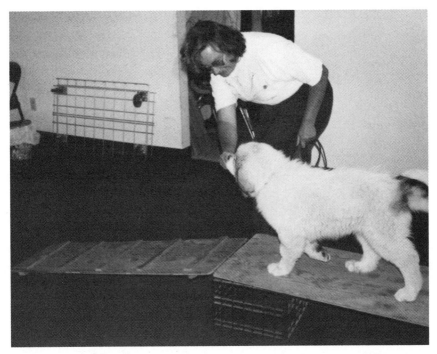

Guide your puppy with a treat at his nose until he gains confidence.
Photo by Author.

and how well he's behaving. Handle the pup's feet every time you groom, and clip nails every week or two.

If you're wishy-washy in your attitude toward grooming and toward having the pup stand still for a minute, your pup will sense this. He will take advantage of you and will never stand still. In this case, you better read the chapter on molding behavior. You might have to give the pup a scruff-shake to make him realize that you're the boss.

Important Basic Information for Teaching Puppies

Here are some basic guidelines that you can adopt as you work with your puppy to teach him good house manners.

Above: A friend is at one end of the tunnel with your puppy while you call from the other. *Photo by Author.*

Below: Sometimes a puppy needs a confidence boost. *Photo by Author.*

Don't Get Tough

Emotionally and psychologically, the pup is extremely sensitive. This means that learning takes place quickly, but that fears can also occur easily and thus inhibit learning. Pups cannot take pressure or harsh treatment. Repetition is the key.

Keep It Simple

A pup learns to do things in a step-by-step manner. If you expect a pup to do something before you've properly taught him to do it, he will lose his confidence and will learn not to try. The same pup, given a simple, step-by-step training approach, will become a dog that is eager to learn and that is ready for more complicated training as he gets older.

Be Brief

Puppies have a very short attention span. A pup learns only while he pays attention to you, and you won't accomplish anything if you keep on training when the pup is mentally tired, even though physically he may still be very lively.

Build Confidence

Relax while you're with the puppy. Smile at him, speak in a pleasant voice, and play running games with him. It's important at this age for the pup to feel that he's a valuable individual. Do your training exercises in a relatively quiet place around the house and yard. Because he's so playful, the pup is easily distracted by other people and activities. If he's constantly being interrupted by other sights and sounds, it will be difficult for him to get the message that you enjoy being with him and that you think he's wonderful.

Use Words

Don't expect your pup to be a mind reader. The only way that he'll learn to associate the command with the action is if you use the word every time you guide him into doing what you want. A puppy can learn a large vocabulary with words such as "outdoors," "bedtime," and "go for a walk," as well as the common commands.

Don't Expect Overnight Results

Try to stay relaxed as you work with the pup. Puppies learn in spurts and starts. One day, he may know absolutely everything and perform to perfection. The next day, it's as though he never had a moment's training. Too many owners make the mistake of thinking that if their puppy does it right once or twice, he knows it forever. But it really takes hundreds of repetitions for a puppy to learn something. He may go through several periods of confusion in the process. You may think that he's mad at you or is trying to spite you. In reality, he's probably trying to tell you that he's confused for some reason. This is often caused by some unknown factor. Perhaps you've done something a little differently, or the environment has changed in some way and his confidence has been shaken. Continue with your training program. It will all iron out with time and effort.

If you take these suggestions into consideration, you are automatically teaching your pup to pay attention. By adhering to his physical and psychological needs, you'll find that he will respond to you, and you will be well on your way to building a good puppy-person relationship.

If you keep repeating the name of a toy you play with, one day your pup will select the one you ask for. *Photo by Author.*

CHAPTER 7

DOMESTICATING YOUR PUPPY:
Shaping Your Pup's Behavior

Barring extremes of shyness or aggressiveness, there is enough
potential variation of behavioral patterns that you'll be able to
modify your puppy's behavior to fit in with your life-style.
You do this by encouraging the characteristics that you like.

Much of a puppy's future behavior is set by what he experiences between three and sixteen weeks of age. His basic attitude toward people and his desire to please are established during these weeks. This chapter discusses the many ways in which new owners will have to mold the behavior of the pup to fit into their life-style. This is the age when the owner and the pup's environment are both having a very strong influence in the development of the puppy's mature personality. Hard work during this period pays big dividends the rest of the dog's life.

Begin Now

It comes as a surprise to many people that their puppy is already developing behavior habits from the day he enters his new home. An example of this is how a puppy can learn to sit for his food dish before he even knows the sit command.

Hold the food dish up, back and over his head. The instant the pup's rear moves in a sitting direction, get the dish to the floor. The first few times you try this, the pup may not look like he's going to sit. Try to time the food dish delivery with a bending of his hind legs. After several days of good timing on your part, the pup will be sitting when he sees you with the food dish. This is

an example of how easily a pup's behavior can be molded, beginning as early as seven weeks of age.

A pup can just as easily be conditioned to bite your pant leg or to bark at you. If your response is to pick him up and hold him in an effort to stop the behavior, the pup perceives this as a reward (even though unintentional on your part) and therefore sees the behavior as acceptable.

A puppy's behavior is constantly being molded all day long in this same manner. Whenever we praise the pup, or pat or cuddle him, the behavior immediately preceding is being *encouraged*. Whenever we speak sharply or distract the pup or discipline him, that behavior is being *discouraged*. Puppies develop habits very quickly. If you can control *your* behavior and pay attention to what actions you're rewarding, you're going to end up with a nice dog that you'll be happy to have around the house. It's much easier to encourage good behavior than to change bad behavior after the puppy has been allowed to get away with it.

The Bonding Process

Bonding occurs most readily between the age of seven to sixteen weeks. To ensure that a pup will be responsive to his owner as well as to other people throughout the rest of his life, he needs to bond to someone at this age. In a puppy's perspective, bonding means that he has someone to respect, to trust, to play with, and to show him what he can and cannot do. He has someone who cares. To you, bonding means that your pup will follow you around the house and look to you for approval of his just being there.

Bonding is the process of putting yourself first in your pup's priorities. It's your pup looking at *you* when you say his name; it's your pup coming to *you* when you call him, rather than running on past. To accomplish this bonding takes time spent one-on-one with your pup, taking walks with your pup, and not giving up if your pup doesn't respond as readily as you think he should. The independent, dominant, or overly busy puppy can reach a high degree of bonding if *you* keep working with him. So don't throw your hands up in impatience.

An excellent way to begin the bonding process is to tether your pup to you. Put your pup on a six-foot leash, and tie it around your waist or through a belt loop. The leash must be long enough for the pup to be able to sit or lie down, but you don't want a cord so long that it lets him wander several feet away from you. As you go about your business around the house, don't give your pup any commands such as sit or down. If he insists on jumping, give a quick, downward tug on the leash close to the collar. Prohibit biting or chewing by a swift bump or a sharp "no!" Tether your

Tethering can be done anywhere around the house.

pup at least twenty minutes (longer if possible) for several days. Your pup is beginning his one-on-one relationship with you. The more independent your pup's personality, the more he needs this process.

Because bonding is in process at this age, you need to give special attention to how you teach your pup about good house manners, and you need to learn what disciplines you should and shouldn't use.

Punishment

There's no place for punishment with young puppies. Hitting a puppy with a newspaper, or spanking with your hand is cruel punishment for *any* misbehavior. It certainly appears to be effective because your pup immediately stops his bad behavior and looks sorry for what he's done (unless he's dominant-aggressive, in which case he might challenge you), but puppies don't understand this punishment. It works against their natural attraction to people. It can build a wall of defense mechanisms that results in a dog that is more difficult to train and to communicate with when he's older. What you've gained in immediate release of your anger, you've lost in your dog's confidence and total trust.

Another abusive discipline is loud, angry, emotional shouting. A human voice with a nasty tone to it can put a touch of panic in your pup's mind, or if he's independent, stubborn or dominant, it can make him turn more into himself, becoming more and more unresponsive to you. Your pup is a baby. The purpose of this book is to help you get your baby dog off to a good start. Your attitude and approach to discipline is part of the bonding process and involves establishing yourself as the alpha member of your puppy's new pack. Puppies do need discipline at times — the right kind of discipline.

A major aspect of the bonding process involves establishing yourself as the alpha member of your puppy's new pack. Your role as pack leader begins when you bring the puppy home, and it is a matter, at this age, of your attitude and approach to discipline.

Discipline

Very few of us live with the perfect puppy. A busy puppy, full of joyful energy, can get himself in trouble because he doesn't know what he can and can't do around the house. We use discipline to correct a puppy's bad (from our point of view) behavior. When we correct a behavior, we are saying to the pup, "I want your attention right now. What you're doing is not okay." We want to halt that behavior, gain his full attention, then show him what behavior we do want from him. Fortunately, a variety of disciplines exist to effectively help the pup understand what behaviors we don't like. Praising our pup's good behavior helps him to understand what behaviors we do like.

Distraction

Distraction followed by praise works very well in molding your pup's behavior. Much of the mischief that a puppy gets into is a result of busyness. Many behaviors, like pulling on drapes or unrolling a roll of toilet paper by running through the house carrying the end of it, are not repeated once the pup has been distracted and gone on to other things.

If your pup is young — seven to ten weeks old — or is especially sound sensitive, use your voice to distract him. A loud "uh-uh" or a hand clap, or a slap on a table to startle the pup, will divert his attention to you. If the pup is ignoring you, use a shake can. For puppies, a Tums™ bottle with a few pennies in it makes an impressive sound to divert a pup's attention from his current mischief. The flat-sided bottle fits nicely into your pocket, making it handy and ready for action. For some pups, you might want to put the pennies in an empty pop can to make a louder distraction. When your pup is involved in a "no-no," shake the can. The startle effect should stop his action. When he looks up in surprise, distract him, talk to him, call him to you (you are very close), and praise him for being a good puppy.

Good behavior consists of simply not doing what he has been doing. If he's *not* doing whatever it was you didn't like, then he must be a good puppy — so tell him. How else will he know? Your praise is calm, not exciting. You are simply telling him that you prefer his good behavior over his bad behavior.

Canine-Type Discipline

To teach a puppy that he can't do "that" anymore, you have to catch him in the act and discipline him. How do adult canids discipline young canids? Primarily by using the element of surprise. When the pup is disciplined the first time — such as for trying to share a bone — the adult dog might snarl and grab for the pup, sometimes pinning him down. The pup is startled so abruptly that he often cries as though he's been mortally wounded. Following that initial discipline, it takes only a curl of the lip or a quiet growl to remind the pup of what not to touch or where not to go. Of course, with some pups, particularly the very lively ones, the discipline wears off rather quickly, and then the pup asks for it again. He is startled into submission, and the cycle of good behavior begins once again.

We can use canine-type discipline to simulate the way adult dogs discipline puppies. This can be very effective if it is done

Puppies first learn discipline from their mother. *Photo by Kent Dannen.*

appropriately. Timing is the essence here, because the element of surprise is a major part of the effectiveness. The scruff-shake is a vigorous discipline, but there are milder disciplines that are easier for many people to accomplish and that can be equally effective. We call these time-out and isolation.

Scruff-Shake. When you catch the puppy in the act, like jumping up on the table, take hold of his scruff under his ear and give a brief but brisk shake. If the puppy is small and has little loose skin under his ear (on the side of his neck), grasp his collar with your thumb and finger and give a quick shake. If the scruff-shake has been quick enough, your puppy should indicate, by ear position or by some degree of submission, that he understands you don't like him jumping on the table (or chewing the lamp cord, etc.). But if he's merrily bouncing around with not a care in the world, you will know that the element of surprise and quickness wasn't there. If you find that this isn't a good discipline for you, don't use it. Other techniques might be more suitable.

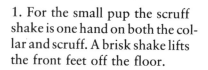

1. For the small pup the scruff shake is one hand on both the collar and scruff. A brisk shake lifts the front feet off the floor.

2. For the older and larger pup, the scruff shake is with both hands. Make eye contact as soon as shake is finished.

Distract the puppy with a toy and take away what he is chewing.
Photo by Beth Baily.

If you find that you are using the scruff-shake frequently, like several times a week, you should evaluate your relationship with your pup. Is he getting enough exercise? Are you spending enough time with him on a one-to-one basis? If you are using the canine-type disciplines often, then they are ineffective and shouldn't be used at all. Don't hesitate to call your breeder or another experienced person for advice.

Other canine disciplines might be more effective for you. These are a natural follow-through from the antisocial behavior that the pup might have experienced in the litter. When a puppy is playing too roughly with his teeth, the puppy that is being chewed on gives a screech and moves away. He won't play anymore. We can imitate this behavior.

Isolation. Isolation is effective because it's an immediate reaction the instant the pup misbehaves. A pup is a very social creature, and you are his adult pack member. If you totally withdraw all attention, he's going to be a very unhappy pup. So — when he's very mouthy and grabs at you when you pet him — say

If your pup plays too rough, isolate him by totally ignoring him until he calms down. *Photo by Sarah Baily. Owner, Sarah Baily.*

"off" or "no bite," and *immediately* turn your back to him. Fold your arms tightly, and even close your eyes. *Do not talk.* If he starts to jump on you or if he starts to bark, totally ignore him. Walk away and leave the room if necessary. The pup should feel completely isolated from you. After about a minute, unfreeze and say "hi" to your puppy. Tell him that he's a good puppy at that moment and that you hope he will continue to be good. Pat him again, and if his mouth starts chewing on you, repeat the isolation. And, of course, repeat the resultant quiet praise. It may take several repetitions in succession, but he should soon get the message.

Time-Out. The other method is called time-out. When your pup is doing something that you don't like — such as grabbing and chewing your pant leg — leave the room for a minute or two, or pick up the pup and take him to his crate or a time-out room (such as the bathroom or the kitchen). Do not shout or use an angry voice. In a minute or two, let him back in, telling him quietly that now he's a good puppy. For extra-lively pups, divert their attention from the unwanted activity with a toy when they come back in. When you use a time-out, don't just go off and leave him there, because then it won't be a learning situation for the pup. Bring the pup back in and repeat the time-out if necessary. Some pups need two or three repetitions in a row before they get the message.

Squirt Bottles. Many owners have success using squirt bottles for discipline. It interrupts the pup in the midst of barking or jumping up or grabbing at hands, and at the same time, the pup hears the "quiet" or "off" command, followed by praise when he is no longer performing that unwanted behavior. Water bottles work well for a few times, but then puppies tend to treat the

The squirt bottle should be held close to the puppy's mouth. Use a stream, not a spray. *Photo by Sarah Baily.*

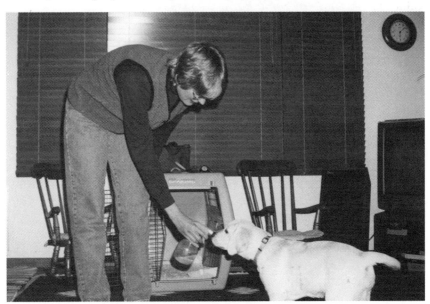

water squirt as a game. A most effective spray is a vinegar solution (one part vinegar to either six or four parts water). Use the stream, not the spray. We have found white vinegar to be effective, but other kinds should work, too. Spray at the mouth area. Vinegar seems to be universally distasteful and therefore a successful inhibitor of certain behaviors for puppies from about three months old on through adulthood.

A squeeze lemon has the same effect on many pups, but some pups get to the point of liking the taste. Still, it's worth a try.

A breath-mint spray in a cartridge, sprayed at the older pup's or dog's mouth, is a sure deterrent to the activity you want to eliminate. This can help convince the vigorous dog that wants to do everything his way that it works better if he listens to you.

The Sit Command. This command is an important part of the disciplinary process. You have given your "no" command to stop the behavior, followed immediately with "sit" to get the pup to respond to you. This is effective because you have not only stopped the bad behavior, you have also given the pup an

Teach the sit command in varying situations.

alternative behavior for which he can then be praised. Obviously, the pup needs to know the sit command well enough to be able to respond to it under varying circumstances.

The No Command. Don't overuse this or your pup will tune it out and it will lose its effectiveness. Decide what bugs you the most and use it for these two or three behaviors. For others, use "uh-uh" or "wrong." Once your pup understands that "no" means to stop what he's doing, you can begin using it more often, in a speaking tone of voice, and he should stop or at least pause at whatever he is doing.

Evaluating the Different Disciplines

Domesticating a puppy involves continual interaction between two individual living beings — the puppy and his owner. We must acknowledge the fact that problems can principally be with the owner as much as with the puppy. In analyzing the effect of your teaching methods (discipline *is* teaching) with your puppy, ask yourself: Is this particular method effective? If not, is *any* method working? If not, then what is wrong?

At this point, take an objective look at your personality and at your pup's personality. Is your pup growing up differently than you had anticipated? Do you sometimes think that you're a mismatch? Puppies go through many phases before they mature. Often, if you patiently keep on doing what you're doing, the pup will grow out of that particularly difficult stage of behavior. Encourage and praise the behaviors that make you happy. Distract or discourage the behaviors that you don't like. This is the way in which you can mold your pup's personality.

When you are evaluating, you must also be aware that there may be an underlying physical or functional abnormality causing the pup's difficult or seemingly intractable behavior. Have your pup checked out by a veterinarian before you proceed.

Puppies Will Be Puppies

There's the possibility that you may inadvertently exaggerate the degree of the behavioral problem of your puppy. Especially with a first puppy, you may not realize that some digging, some chewing, some barking, and some jumping up are natural. This is why we keep stressing that it's up to you, as the owner, to teach the puppy what to do and what not to do. Puppies are canids, and there are certain behaviors that are simply not wrong from the puppy's point of view. So don't get angry at the pup just because you decide that he should act more like a person than a dog. Simply get busy and show him what you want him to do and what you don't want him to do.

Molding your pup's behavior isn't done in a day or two. It takes weeks of praising good behavior and discouraging bad behavior. It's a style of living — a daily program. Repeating your lesson in as many new places as you can will help you and your puppy learn to live together. Lessons learned at home will need to be repeated elsewhere so that the puppy learns what behavior you want and not just that the rules apply in your own house.

Accept your puppy as he is, not as you think he should be. If your pup is shy, it won't help for you to get stern and impatient. Accept the shyness and do what needs to be done. This also applies to the independent puppy and the assertive puppy. Over a period of weeks, you will find that confidence and communication between the two of you are increasing and that your pup's general behavior is changing to your mutual satisfaction.

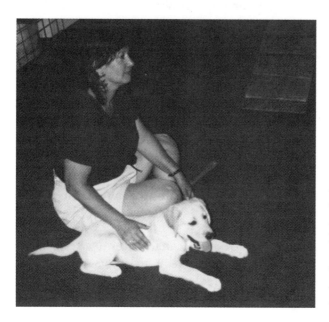

A puppy down stay means having your puppy learn to be quiet at your side.
Photo by Author.

CHAPTER 8

DEVELOPMENT FROM THREE TO SIX MONTHS

This is an age to enjoy — but watch out! Your puppy is NOT too good to be true.

The rapid changes noticeable in the puppy's behavior during the first three months have leveled off. The central nervous system is now well-developed. By three months of age, the pup's problem-solving ability is functioning well, but his immaturity gets in the way. In other words, he has a short attention span and is too rambunctious to settle down and learn complicated behavior. However, he's certainly ready to learn simple commands (as discussed in Chapter 6).

This a delightful age and passes much too quickly. By the end of this period, the large-breed pups have grown to approximately two-thirds of their mature size, and small breeds may be close to their final height. After six months of age, the puppy will become much more independent, will reach sexual maturity, and will be very responsive to physiological stimuli. However, the age from three to six months is still one of puppy charm and innocence. The pup and people are adjusting to each other, and the pup is learning what the pack rules are. He's readily able to cope with life by now, he's a willing worker, and he is happy to try whatever you ask (at least most of the time).

Taking the pup to different places continues to be important at this age. The pup's environmental awareness is at a peak now. He's ready for anything. Exposure to a variety of places will continue to be a factor in building self-confidence in the puppy and will help him take stressful events in the future in his stride.

The second set of teeth begins to appear during this period, which can cause chewing and biting problems. The puppy needs some items of his own for chewing.

Dominance and Submission

By four months of age, the pup is beginning to show signs of dominance and submissiveness toward other dogs. Previously, we noted that a young puppy shouldn't be left with irritable older dogs because the puppy wouldn't recognize the dominance signs of the older dog and wouldn't respond with a sign of submission. As a consequence, the pup might get bitten. However, around four months of age, this changes, and the pup becomes aware that dominance is displayed by direct eye contact, by a tail held straight up and tightly moving, by a growl and showing of the front teeth, and by the dominant dog's putting his head over the shoulder area of the other dog.

The submissive signs that the pup will display toward a dominant dog are a flattening of the ears, tucking the tail between the legs, and cowering, if not rolling over on the side or back. Usually, a puppy is submissive to an older dog, although in some instances a very assertive puppy will soon realize that he can be dominant to an especially submissive adult. With young dogs close in age, some pups will be dominant over others, and generally a dominant-

Young dogs display dominance by leaning over the other dog. Note erect ears and high tail.

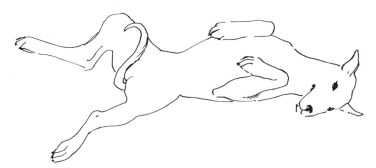

Total submissiveness can be demonstrated to either another dog or a person. Note tucked tail and averted gaze.

submissive relationship is established very quickly. With some pups, it's a change-about situation as they take turns at dominance and submission.

Avoidance Period

Around four months of age, the pup will go through an avoidance period similar to the fear period experienced at eight weeks. The

puppy becomes very hesitant about doing anything new and different and becomes quite suspicious of anything new that is brought
into his home environment or of any new place that he might be
visiting.

If your pup has a quiet personality, he may not respond as
happily during training sessions, or he may seem hesitant and a
little fearful if you take him to a new place. If this is the case, ease
off the training routine. Make it fun; just enjoy being with your pup.

On the other hand, if you have a very independent or assertive
pup, this age may find him in a relatively receptive frame of mind.
His being a little apprehensive of new things in his life will tend
to make him look to you for support. While he's paying attention
to you, get busy and teach him something.

Teething

In many breeds, there can be retention of puppy teeth during
the period that permanent teeth are erupting. This can have a
long-lasting effect in that the pathway that the permanent teeth
will take if the puppy teeth are retained will be abnormal and may
lead to permanent problems with the way in which the teeth close
together. Another problem associated with retention of puppy teeth
is damage to the surrounding gum, which may progress to chronic
oral disease in adult life. Bearing in mind that the pup between
four and five months is extra-sensitive, you should pay careful
attention to the possibility of teething problems. If you have any
doubts that teething is not going well, consult your veterinarian
immediately.

The Leadership Concept

In the three- to six-month age period, the most important help
that you can give your puppy is to let him know that you're the
leader. The pup as a new member of the family transfers dependency from his mother to you. If the balance of this relationship
is to be sustained, you must maintain the dominant role in your
puppy's life.

Pups need to play with many different dog friends.
Photo by James Digby.

The dog is not a democratic animal. If you allow your pup an equal say in his activities, he will interpret that as permission to do whatever he wants. He will begin to guide your activities to coincide with his benefits. He'll determine such things as where he wants to sleep, how often he wants to be let in and out of the house, and how much attention he gets. A dog with a more aggressive personality may even go to the extent of not letting you touch his food or growling or snapping if you try to make him do something that he doesn't want to do.

An extremely important and necessary factor in raising a puppy is to establish your dominance. This involves a conscious effort on your part. It's very easy to let these three months slide by and to think that *your* puppy doesn't need training because he's such a good dog. But in a few months, you'll regret that decision. The sweet puppy that never needed puppy training because he never did anything wrong begins to exercise his mature personality. He's not mean, but suddenly he's a lively handful that isn't paying attention to you because the pattern of communication wasn't established as a puppy. This applies to the toy breeds as well as to the large breeds. Three to six months is a good age to reinforce your dominant role. Because the pup still wants to be close to you, it's easy to get his attention and he's easy to discipline.

The Dominant Family Member

Anyone who has been involved in maintaining a small group of dogs together in a common environment will know that they establish a social order that has a leader. Because your dog is a dog, he is very aware of social order and will find his position sooner or later in the family situation. Many people assume that they are the dominant leader on the uncertain premise of human supremacy over animals. But are you *really* the leader, and does your dog know it? Many behavioral problems can occur if you're not the leader. There can be more than one leader in the family, but these are adults. Children aren't the family leader but should have the respect of the dog.

Dogs can experience emotional reactions. They experience frustration when they don't know who is in control of their territory and when they don't know which of their actions are acceptable and which are not. Depending on the dog's personality, this uncertainty might manifest itself in the dog's taking over as the leader to the point of growling and snapping or of urinating and defecating in the house after he has been well housetrained.

We feel that it is vitally important for people to understand the leader concept. Establishing the rules of the game can be done easily during puppyhood. It results in a dog that fits into the lifestyle of your home. If minor behavioral problems subsequently arise, they are relatively easy to deal with if you and the dog have developed a mutual respect.

The role of leader is abdicated by many people because they see it as the lion-tamer-with-a-whip concept, or as a dictator complex with no pleasant communication allowed. This is not the case at all. In a good dog-person relationship (with you as the dominant member), mutual respect is absolutely necessary.

The person must respect the dog and must understand the physical and social needs unique to being a canid. On the other hand, the dog must respect you, and he will if he is treated with consistency and if he knows the rules that you have established are for his benefit. Dogs need guidelines and need to know the limits.

How Do You Become the Dominant Leader?

It isn't a short-term battle of wills in which you are the victor and the puppy is vanquished. It is built on daily routine. Being the leader doesn't mean that you must be big and aggressive. A small woman can be the dominant member. It's an attitude — an air of authority. It's the basis for the mutual respect that is so important for building a bridge of communication between the two of you.

Many dominance activities are a part of the puppy training routine (which is discussed in detail in Chapter 11). "Sit" is the most important command that your pup can learn because it is so easy to use as a reminder that you're in charge of things. Tell the pup to "sit" before you feed him, before you play with him, and before you let him go outside. This shows the pup that he must respond to you before he indulges in pleasure for himself and keeps him from becoming a spoiled brat.

As you're teaching him the sit, praise him with a pat on the chest, which is in itself a means of impressing your leadership position on the puppy. Leaning over is canine language for dominance. (In fact, if you have an especially sensitive or shy puppy, you may want to avoid leaning over the pup because it may intimidate him.)

Another good leader exercise involves combining the come with taking the pup on a walk without a leash. For this, you should take the puppy to an area that's uncrowded, preferably with no people at all. Most three-month-old pups won't want to get too far away from you, which is another reason why this is a good age. Go for a walk together, and when the pup gets about twenty-five feet away, get his attention by calling his name and clapping your hands. When he looks at you, kneel down and call him to you. Give him lots of praise when he gets to you and continue your walk, repeating this another three or four times. If

Above: Walking with a pup helps put you in the role of leader. *Photo by James Digby.*
Below: Periodically stop and call him to you. *Photo by James Digby.*

Retractable leads work well for exercising dogs. With puppies, stop often for short breaks. *Photo by Scott Baily.*

you have an independent puppy that ignores you, try running away from him. Many pups can't resist that and will follow. If you have a *very* independent puppy, begin calling him when he's no more than eight to ten feet away and give him a small piece of cheese or some other good treat as soon as he gets to you. This exercise reminds the puppy that you're always there and that you're the leader who must be reported to every so often.

You'll be accepted as the family leader by your dog when you're consistent and fair in your demands. For example, if you let the pup jump up on you one day and the next day you kick or slap him for doing the same thing, the pup will be confused and will wonder when he can do something and when not.

The dominant family leader doesn't permit the puppy to growl or snap at him. A severe scruff-shaking or time out is necessary when this happens, followed by no attention from you for ten to fifteen minutes. A growl or a snap is not unusual behavior for many pups. It's a natural way for them to show irritation. Usually one or two corrections are all that's necessary to eliminate that behavior. However, if the pup is not corrected, you're asking for big trouble later. Give some thought as to what stimulus provoked the growl or the snap. If the pup has been treated unnecessarily roughly, it's up to you to change the situation.

How Does a Dog Become the Dominant Leader?

Very easily. He's either ignored most of the time or overindulged and smothered with attention. He isn't trained. He isn't taught the difference between good and bad and so he establishes is own criteria with himself as the center of attention. As a result, he may become not very pleasant for you or your friends and neighbors to live with. It's supposed to be the other way around — the dog is living in *your* world. Someone has to call the shots, and both you and your dog will be happier if it's you.

Conclusion

Guide the puppy to behave the way you want him to from the time you bring him home. Be patient. Behavior development takes time. If you're relaxed and don't turn every act of your puppy into a major battle, you'll find that having a puppy in the house is one of the most delightful experiences you've ever had and that having a mature dog in the house that respects you is deeply rewarding.

CHAPTER 9

THE IMPORTANCE OF PERSONALITY

*"Accept your puppy as he is, then mold
the kind of dog you want."*

Sometimes it's very difficult to see your pup as he really is, rather than as you want him to be. Exuberant, forceful people cannot really believe that their pup might be a little short of confidence and need morale-boosting. Quiet people have difficulty believing that their pup is leader-oriented and must have a firm hand and firm voice. Surely, this assertive little puppy will become sweet and gentle any day now — wishing will make it so. The fact is, you must accept the pup the way he is and then proceed to mold the kind of adult dog you want.

Individual Characteristics

The pup's individual genetic qualities determine factors such as the degree of shyness or aggressiveness and other traits such as curiosity and excitability. These traits are found in all breeds, purebred and mongrel alike, and are components in a dog's personality. What is the basic temperament of your puppy? Is he dependent, independent, leader-oriented, aggressive, eager to please, shy, or too easily excited? As the pack leader, you will continue to develop a communication with your pup by training him. This needs to be done according to the pup's personality, however, or the training can do more harm than good at this age.

The Dependent Puppy

This pup is usually found in the toy breeds. He looks to his owner for approval for all of his actions and tends to be emotional. This pup wants constantly to stay very close to his owner and does a minimum of investigating. It's very easy to get in the habit of carrying this puppy, an activity that should be limited because it will exaggerate the dog's dependency to the extent of making him overly nervous. Gentleness is needed in living with this pup. Keep showing the pup what you expect him to do, and he'll soon respond. Don't treat this pup like a baby. That will make him an emotional cripple. Just because he's small and acts very dependent upon you doesn't mean that he can't learn good puppy behavior.

The Independent Puppy

A little independence is a good thing. There is nothing wrong with having a puppy that thinks for himself at times, but some pups are more inclined this way than others. The sign of a very independent puppy is to not be able to get his attention to come to you when you are only six feet away calling him. This pup will ignore your voice and your hand clapping and will sniff along, going his own merry way. If this pup isn't given puppy training, he will be difficult to train as an adult because his desire to please will by then be focused mostly on himself. This pup takes patience and firmness but generally is easy to train because the dog is calm and not emotional.

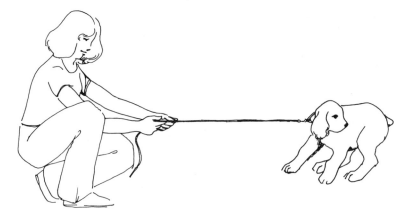

Use a cord to keep the independent puppy under control during the training sessions so that he can never not come when called.

If it's possible, keep the pup in a dog crate or in a room or yard area by himself for at least thirty minutes before the training session. This will help to encourage his attention to you. If at first he seems more interested in everything else than in you, be patient and show him firmly what you want him to do. Reward him with a pat on the chest or with your voice, saying, "Good dog," or both. You may want to use tidbits to get his attention. The trick is to keep his attention zeroed in on you. Keep sessions short and be aware that it might take many of them before your pup responds like you want him to.

The Eager-to-Please Puppy

This pup will respond to your voice very quickly and will eagerly come running to you when you call him (from close distances, of course). It will seem as though he learns very quickly because he wants to do what you show him to do. He's so responsive to you that it's easy to mistake this and think that he already knows how to sit or come or stay. However, this pup needs much repetition and will take almost as long to actually learn something as the more independent puppy. This is probably the easiest type to work with. Training sessions can be for longer periods without stressing the puppy. But to begin with, no pup should have more than five minutes at a time. These pups are filled with charm and will train you readily to their desires, so watch for this.

The Shy Puppy

This pup has some distinctive behavioral patterns. He may crouch and freeze when you approach him. He may be overly sensitive. He may cringe and stay away if you raise your voice even a little. He may be very fearful in a new place, even though there are no noises or other frightening things. He may not want to approach another person even though the person is quiet and nonfrightening. Some pups will roll on their sides or urinate when you show them attention. This is also an indication of excessive submission.

Guide the puppy gently but firmly to do what you want him to do, then follow a couple of minutes of working with a short play period. Improvement will be slow, but it will come. The pup may not want to participate in learning any of the commands such as sit or come or stay, but keep repeating the learning sessions with lots of patience.

You must be the pack leader for this puppy also. If you're not, the pup will take over the job. He can see that he has you trained to let him act the way he wants. For example, if you feel sorry for this pup when he starts to act shy and frightened and you begin to pet him, you are rewarding his behavior and encouraging him to act that way in the future. Instead, when he begins to act shy,

A pup showing signs of submissiveness.

speak to him in a pleasant, firm voice, but don't pet him until his behavior is more what you want it to be, even if for only a split second. It is especially important to make the training sessions fun. Keep his mind on you and off himself.

This pup was born with a short supply of confidence, and he will need a lot of patience from you. His behavior will gradually improve as your pup gets confidence in himself and in you.

The Dominant Puppy That Competes for Pack Leadership

The dominant-aggressive pup is a very active one and demands a lot of attention. He's little and cute, and it's very easy to give him all of the attention that he wants. He becomes spoiled because of the overindulgence. Then the aggressive tendency shows up as he grows older and you don't want to cater to him anymore. He will let you know that he's unhappy with you.

The competitive puppy might snap at you if you reach down to move his feed pan while he's eating, or he may snap at you during leash training if he decides that he doesn't want to stay at your side. In other words, the pup will try to do things his way, and if you permit this, you are setting yourself up for serious, difficult behavior as he gets older. Aggressive actions in the puppy cannot be permitted. We can't stress strongly enough the importance of not allowing the aggressive puppy to become the dominant member of the relationship.

When the pup snaps at you, it will be a shock and a surprise, but don't retreat, because this is what he wants. This rewards his snapping and encourages him to do it again. Use a severe scruff-shake or be prepared with a squirt bottle of vinegar water. When this type of puppy needs to be disciplined, he shouldn't be slapped or beaten, because he might take it as a challenge and fight back.

Puppy training is essential for the leader-oriented pup. It teaches him that he receives a reward for obeying, for submitting to your commands. Teach the pup the sit command and use it constantly. This keeps reminding the pup that you're the boss.

The Extremely Excitable Puppy

All puppies can become excited easily, but some won't calm down. Some you can hardly touch because they are constantly wiggling. Such a pup will really try your patience. He's difficult

The curious puppy is always busy. *Photo by Kent Dannen.*

to work with because you can't get his attention for more than a few seconds. You may need to start with sessions that are less than a minute long. They can gradually become longer as the pup learns to pay attention. Try not to add to his excitement by any quick motions on your part. Stay calm with as little body movement as possible. Keep repeating the training routine. Don't pet him or tell him that he's a good dog until you've finished the training session. Sometimes it helps if the pup is allowed to run off some of his energy in a supervised enclosure before the training lesson begins. Then put the leash on and tell him that school is in session.

If over a period of time you've tried the puppy training routine every day and you see no improvement, there may be a physiological reason for the pup's behavior. In a few cases, some pups are so excitable that you can't hold their attention long enough to even begin training. These are signs of overexcitability, in which case you should get the help of a veterinarian. Certain dogs have a problem similar to hyperactive children and respond to similar treatment. If you think that this might be the case, discuss it with your veterinarian.

The Trainer's Personality

Your personality is also a factor in puppy training. If you are very shy — or quite assertive — this may indeed affect your pup's reactions to you. Be aware of how you are coming across to your pup. If necessary, moderate your approach. Usually, though, a pup will adjust to your individual personality and will want to do things your way as long as you're consistent and he knows what you want him to do. Within the bounds of respecting your pup and not abusing him, your method of dog training should be what seems natural to you. It's up to you to decide if you're being too tough on your pup or too lenient. Be honest with yourself. Open your eyes. Your pup is continually telling you how things really are and what kind of training he needs from you. Puppy training is a one-on-one proposition. Trust your instincts. Listen to your pup; read his body language. He can tell you a lot more than your neighbor can.

As different as breed and genetic characteristics might be in a population of puppies, almost any one of them, if given adequate socialization, can learn to respond to humans in a very satisfactory way.

Photo by Judith Strom.

CHAPTER 10

BEHAVIORAL PROBLEMS

*Don't let your pup learn bad habits! That's the cardinal
rule of the right start.*

You have probably noticed that your pup has behavioral problems in which he specializes. Some puppies seem to have a preference in where they want to channel their mischief. In this chapter, we will talk about ideas for dealing with specific puppy behaviors that you want to stop. You can and should expect your pup to learn good behavior!

Most behavioral problems are caused by boredom and isolation. This is why we say that it is essential to spend time every day with your pup and have him with you in the house or in the yard while you're home. When you're not home, the pup should not be loose in the house but should be either in a crate, in a small puppy-proof room, or in an outdoor pen.

Prevention of Behavioral Problems

A few problem behaviors don't become noticeable until the pup reaches adolescence. By that time, it's more difficult to deal with the problem than it would have been to prevent it earlier. When problem behaviors do appear in earlier puppyhood, start dealing with them right away. Don't put them off and hope that they will go away, because in all probability, they will just get worse. Fortunately, strategies for prevention of problems involve very little time and are easily incorporated into activity time that you would already be spending with your pup.

Guarding the Food Dish

All family members should work on the food-dish exercise at one time or another. This exercise not only prevents your pup from becoming protective of his food, it also accustoms him to having hands come close to his face. This is important if there are children in the family.

There are three things that you can do while your puppy is eating. Begin by putting tidbits into his dish, one at a time, until he's accustomed to your hand reaching out toward his dish. The treat should be something special, such as raw hamburger or pieces of hot dog. You want him to associate a hand in his food dish with something very pleasant. After he has become very comfortable with your hand in his dish, touch his pan, moving it out of position. Finally, pick up his dish and set it back down. If your pup is starting to guard his toys, offer a tidbit while you take his bone or toy from him. This conditions him to accepting your hand. If he growls at any time use a vigorous scruff-shake or vinegar squirt bottle, and give a "No!"

Jumping Out of Reach

It's very natural for a puppy to scoot out of reach when you bend over to take him by the collar. Use a yummy tidbit for this also. Whenever you call your puppy to you, give him a treat with

Reach out and scratch your pup under the ears at every opportunity. This is especially important for both the timid and the dominant puppy because it removes their sense of being threatened when a hand comes towards them.

one hand while the other hand touches his collar. In this way, he'll be comfortable with your hand reaching for his collar. Be sure that your pup comes all the way to you before he receives his treat — don't reach out to him.

Separation Distress

Conditioning your pup to being left home alone can prevent serious problems. If not attended to, separation distress can develop into separation anxiety, which is often expressed by frantic barking and destructiveness. In extreme cases, this can involve furniture or even walls and doors. Conditioning your pup to being left home alone can avoid these problems as your pup grows older. We periodically meet with dog owners who have this problem. It could have been avoided by dealing with this distress when the pup was young, which is the easy time to work with it. Otherwise, by the time a dog reaches adolescence, it is a serious problem indeed.

If your puppy has had constant attention since he first arrived at your home, and then you suddenly leave him home alone, he can experience a state of isolation that results in fear and panic. Therefore, you need to help your pup learn to be comfortable by himself. Teaching the pup that it's okay to be alone should be done while *you're* at home, too. If the pup is to be left in a small room or the backyard while you're gone, put him there occasionally while you're at home working around the house.

Begin with short separation periods of five minutes. If he's barking when you're ready to return to him, try to wait until he has stopped (at least long enough to take a breath), then open the door. Gradually increase the length of time before you return.

The manner in which you leave the house and later return to your puppy is also a factor in how he perceives your absence. If you're emotional and feel guilty about leaving him, he'll sense this and will become nervous and upset. Practice your arrivals and departures at the same time you're conditioning him to your absence. When you leave him, don't be emotional — no petting or special fun games. Such handling followed immediately by separation can result in more intense separation distress. Keep your departure low-key. You can speak to your pup and tell him that you're leaving, then leave. Use the same phrase every time you leave; for example, "Be a good dog; I'll be back." When you arrive home, greet your pup warmly but briefly and go about your business. Later, when you have time, you can have a play period, take a walk, or whatever.

If your absences are occasional and are for no more than a few hours at a time, the pup's crate is ideal and should not result in distress because that's his den and he is accustomed to it. But all puppies should be taught that they can stay home alone for longer periods of time. Try to have a larger safe area for your puppy if you'll be gone longer than a few hours. Make sure that there's a place where he can eliminate and a shelter place in case of bad weather if he's outdoors.

Digging

There's no magic answer here. It's not your puppy's fault that you have a perfectly landscaped backyard. Sniffing and digging in the dirt are naturally doggy things to do, especially for puppy dogs.

If you can't be out with the pup all the time to distract him when he begins digging, fix a fenced area where he is free to dig all he desires. When you see him digging in another part of the lawn, take him to his own area. Some pups will learn to like digging in their own place, especially if there's a hole already started or the ground is soft. Most puppies outgrow digging, but some mature dogs will periodically dig all their lives. The earth is cool, and the burying of bones is a strong impulse with them. Boredom is another continuing cause of digging.

Specific Behavioral Problems

Chewing

Puppies chew for three reasons: they are bored and want something to do, they have too much energy from not enough exercise, and/or they are teething and have sore gums. You will need to teach your puppy that chewing on his toys is the only chewing allowed. This is the process that we call molding your pup's behavior and is discussed in the previous chapter. For many puppies, this keeps problem chewing to a minimum; however, there's always an item or two around the house that they can't resist, and there is also that percentage of pups that are exceptionally mouthy.

For problem chewers, a bad taste often inhibits the chewing desire. Try Bitter Apple™, available in pet-supply stores, or try very hot Chinese or Mexican pepper sauce. Listerine© and its aroma can be a repellant to pups. Test the furniture or other pieces with a small amount to be certain that no discoloration occurs. Puppies are very sensitive to a distasteful substance and should quickly associate that with the item on which it has been applied. Keep applying the substance until the puppy is no longer testing the area to see if the taste has changed. Be consistent!

Puppies are at their worst between four to six months of age, during the teething process, but the problem can continue periodically for several more months. Some pups find relief with chewing an ice cube or a frozen rawhide chip. To avoid serious chewing damage, never give your pup the run of the house. He should either be with you so that you can monitor his chewing, or he should be confined. Tether the pup to you with a leash or other cord. Then he can be with you when you're too busy to keep track of him all the time. Too many valuables have been ruined because the pup's owner wanted to be "nice."

Barking

Now is the time to develop a pattern of control for barking. This is probably one of the most frustrating problems facing a dog owner. It can create enemies of neighbors and can result in warnings and fines from dog-control agencies — and justifiably so. Any dog that won't stop barking for long periods of time is causing much distress for numerous innocent people and is contributing to anti-dog sentiment. The responsible dog owner begins avoiding this problem by training his puppy to the quiet command.

Barking is a natural canine activity. There's no reason to expect a dog never to bark, but you *can* expect him to learn to stop barking. The shake can is a good way to accomplish this. When the pup has barked a few times, give the quiet command, *then* shake the can until the barking stops. The noise should startle the puppy into silence, at which point you immediately praise him! The pup will likely begin barking again, and you will repeat the procedure as many times as necessary until the pup doesn't return to barking. Always give the command first, then the distraction. *Always* praise the pup as soon as he stops barking.

You also might want to attract him away from where he is barking so that you can achieve success with the quiet command. This is an ongoing process. Some pups learn the quiet command quickly, while others have regular relapses. As with many other aspects of puppy behavior, you automatically work on the problem every time it occurs until you reach a point where you say, "Wow, he's learning that command really well!"

The puppy that is barking outside at night shouldn't be outside all night. He should be in the house, in a crate or in a secure area.

The cause of some barking problems is similar to the cause of some excessive chewing and digging problems — not enough time spent with the puppy, and not enough exercise for the puppy.

Jumping Up

One serious behavioral problem is when the pup — or the dog — jumps on or chases children. Young children have an erratic gait, which can trigger an automatic chase response in the dog's brain. Therefore, he must be taught that this is forbidden. The off command (which means to keep all feet off of humans) can be used for this. Use it consistently whenever the pup tries to jump on anybody. Eventually, the off command, when used at an appropriate time, will stop the pup before he jumps.

You will need to help your pup understand what this command means. When the pup jumps on you, give a quick shake with his collar as you say "Off!" As soon as he's on the floor, tell him that he's a good puppy. Be ready to repeat this several times in a row if necessary. For the larger or older pup, catch the front feet as he jumps, give an off command, then hold him up on his hind feet a few seconds. Praise him after he's back on the floor.

The ideal method, once your puppy knows the sit command, is to tell him to sit, then give him a treat or a pat as soon as his bottom touches down. Isolation often works well with this, too. When he jumps, say "Off!" then turn away and fold your arms across your chest, totally ignoring the puppy. Praise and pet him when he's down on the floor. Don't wait until your pup has jumped on you, then gotten down, to praise good behavior. Give him pats and praise when he's with you and is *not* jumping.

To teach the pup about jumping on children, have the pup on his leash, or make a long line out of clothes line or other cord. Tie the leash around your waist or through your belt. This ensures that you will have instant control for correcting your pup's behavior. Set aside a time for this activity during a play period. When your child comes close and the pup starts to run and jump, give the off command, followed by a quick tug on the leash. Then take hold of the collar and give a brisk shake. Praise him as soon as he's on the ground and being good. If he immediately jumps up, repeat the correction and then the praise.

After your pup begins to understand and is seldom jumping up as long as he's tied to you, continue the training by letting the leash drag on the ground. You will be staying close. As soon as he behaves, praise him with "you're a good dog," and walk near the child again. You may need three or four corrections in succession before the pup settles down. You will also need to repeat this setup for several days in succession and again in about a week.

The child must also be taught how to behave — no screaming or shouting or waving the arms around.

Mouthiness and Biting

A dog feels the world through his mouth. The mouth — the teeth, the cheeks, and the tongue — is a tactile area. If you watch a mature dog, you might see him mouth an item to identify it or understand it. With your puppy, this natural tendency can sometimes get out of hand. If the pup were still in the litter or playing with other dogs, he would be told when he was biting or mouthing too hard. Now that the pup is living in your pack, you will replace the interaction that the pup would have with the other pups and dogs. You must step in and continue with bite-inhibition training in a manner that is perceived as normal by your puppy.

Teach your pup the stop-it or no-bite command. When he nips at you, take him by the collar and look him in the eye for several seconds while you repeat the command. Release him and in a few seconds tell him quietly that he's a good puppy. Reach out to touch him, and if he starts playing with his mouth again, repeat the correction.

Another effective correction is to isolate the pup — totally ignore him as soon as you say "No bite!" Fold your arms, and don't even look at him. After a couple of minutes, give your pup another chance to play with you. Repeat the isolation routine as often as necessary until he moderates his mouthiness.

Occasionally, a puppy owner needs to wear a glove to help teach the pup about biting. With a glove, you can keep your hand movements slow and calm. Often it is the jerky hand movements (because of the sharp teeth) that excite the puppy and keep him grabbing the hand in play.

The glove can also be used to teach your pup the easy or the gentle command so that you can put your hand in the pup's mouth and he won't bite down. *All puppies must learn this command, whatever their breed.*

The Aggressive Puppy

Occasionally, there is a pup that bites not in play but out of fear or dominance aggression. This demands a big "NO" with

All pups should learn the "gentle" or "easy" command. *Photo by Jane Exon.*

your voice. The swiftness of the correction is imperative. Do not talk to the pup after this correction for several minutes.

In the adult dog, aggression is the single most serious behavioral problem with veterinarians and trainers. It's normal for a pup to have an aggressive reaction to some action that he perceives as threatening to him.

However, we emphasized previously that early socialization is very important in familiarizing your puppy with the variety of circumstances that he will encounter in life. If your puppy has had a well-balanced relationship with his littermates until weaning, this bodes well for his ability to interact with dogs in the future. If your puppy has been handled kindly by yourself and by other members of the family — young and old, male and female — this bodes well for future transactions with people. Subsequently, as the puppy passes through the period of environmental awareness (nine to twelve weeks), his understanding of dominance and submission is enhanced. He becomes increasingly aware of his environment and really begins to appreciate what a neat person you are. Finding and establishing the right balance of dominant and submissive behavior throughout these stages will result in a more confident and socially well-adjusted puppy. These are the puppies that will be less likely to give you problems with aggressive behavior. In fact, many of the early problems with fear and dominance-cued aggression will be reduced or prevented by your diligently following the full socialization program.

The pup must learn that any aggressive act will be totally inhibited. Certain cues, such as rapid movement of hands toward the pup, can elicit an aggressive response. These pups must be conditioned to hand movement immediately. With a tidbit in one hand, let the pup nibble and lick while the other hand moves toward the pup's ear. If the pup stops nibbling and eyes the hand, move the hand back. Keep moving forward with one hand (the other is holding the tidbit in front of the pup's mouth) until you can scratch behind the ear and pet the pup. Then reverse hands and repeat the same procedure. At this point, it is essential to teach the gentle, or easy, command, beginning with the gloved hand and progressing to putting your bare hand in the mouth. If this isn't done during the puppy months, very serious problems lie ahead. In addition, puppy training is essential for this pup. This builds self-confidence in the fearful pup and develops an appropriate relationship with the dominant puppy.

Be Creative

No book can possibly cover all of the various and unique problems that puppies present. As you get to know your puppy, you will learn what types of disciplines are more effective, as well as what types of distractions work best. You can utilize this knowledge to determine your own ideas for behavioral problems. Adolescent puppies can certainly keep us on our toes when it comes to staying one jump ahead of their busy minds.

Perhaps your pup is jumping up and getting things off of the kitchen counter. You need to stop this behavior immediately. If you can catch him at it the first times he tries it, your chances of extinguishing the behavior are very good. Use your imagination and think of a setup that will startle him. For example, put some food on a piece of newspaper on the counter. Stack some empty cans around the back and sides of the food. When his paws get on the counter, the paper will move, which will send the cans tumbling. At the same time, you're going to appear from behind a door, saying, "No! Off!" After he's been impressed with the results of his behavior, you can tell him that you much prefer him to keep all of his feet on the floor, and that he's a good boy when he does that.

Teaching your pup the rules of the house is an ongoing, day-by-day process. The weeks of teaching good manners can be very rewarding as you watch the pup blossom with a sense of confidence. The weeks will also be filled with humor and good times, and the occasional times of total frustration will be kept to a minimum.

Here's a suggestion. When you do reach a point of frustration, give some thought to the various aspects of the pup's irritating behavior. Where do your actions fit in? Your pup is acting in accordance with his dog genes. It's your responsibility to understand this and to understand his need for consistency in your behavior. After all, you're the mature, reasoning individual in this growing relationship — aren't you?

Conditioning your puppy to hands in his food bowl prevents growling and guarding of his food when he matures. *Photo by Scott Baily.*

Trading a treat for a toy prevents snapping in the future. Return the toy within a few seconds. *Photo by Scott Baily.*

CHAPTER 11

THE REWARDS OF
PUPPY TRAINING

*The one most important factor in raising and training a
puppy from three to six months of age is getting the puppy
to pay attention to you.*

Just as the mature canids show their pups how to pay attention and how to behave in the pack, so now the human must show the pup how to pay attention and behave as a new member of the human pack. This is puppy training — teaching a pup how to be a happy, cooperative member of his human pack.

You may think that this training isn't necessary for *your* pup. He's so attentive and does everything that you want him to do. Please, take it on faith that he needs to learn the basics of how to concentrate and how to do basic tasks on command while it's still easy for you both. When your pup is around six months of age and older, he'll want to do *what* he wants to do and *when* he wants to do it. If you have a communication system going by then, you'll be able to minimize some of the major frustrations, such as running through the house, jumping on people and furniture, tracking every interesting smell, and, most of all, ignoring you. Female pups are just as good at this as males.

Communicating with Your Puppy

The tasks that you teach in puppy training are the foundation for communication as your puppy ventures into adolescence. You want to bring out the best in your puppy. You want him to relate to you, to your family, to your veterinarian, and to your friends. The basis for a relationship between you and your puppy is built through the use of your hands, your eyes, your voice, and the leash.

Using Hands for Communication

The first contact with human hands is in the whelping box, where the pup is picked up and handled as part of the daily routine — with a certain amount of cuddling, too. These hands move with confidence, and the stroking gives the puppy a feeling of security.

After you take the pup to your home, your hands will calm the puppy, warm him, play with him, and let him know that he can have confidence in his new pack home. However, as the pack leader, you must take care that his attitude toward hands doesn't change. Hands sometimes come at the puppy too often and too abruptly (especially if there are children in the family), and the pup might growl or snap or shy away. To prevent this, you can teach your puppy that hands are okay, that even though the movement might be quick and startling, these are human hands and should be accepted as a fact of life. You are also responsible to see that the pup is never *abused* by hands.

The way in which you use your hands during the pup's socialization determines how that pup will react to your hands. He has to learn how to read your hand movements. To begin conditioning your pup to hand movements, use tiny tidbits. Have them in your

Above: Continue to use voice and hand communication as your puppy grows. Keep the pup's attention on you. Use your voice. Pat your leg. *Below:* Get your pup's attention the moment he becomes distracted. *Photos by Joyce Woolley.*

pocket, and occasionally when your pup is close to you, offer a tidbit. While he is sniffing and taking it, reach out for his collar with your other hand, or touch his ear, or pat him on the head. As he gets accustomed to taking tidbits, move your hand more quickly. Each member of the family should do this individually.

When you begin teaching basic commands such as the sit, become very aware of where that hand is. Does it stay in the appropriate position, or does it wave about randomly as though the hand muscles are not under your control? Many of you will be surprised to find how erratic your hand movements are — over and around and anywhere but next to the pup's lips and nose — which is where your hand should be when you begin the teaching process. Any other movement can be distracting or confusing to the pup. The details of hand position and movement will be discussed in the instructions for teaching the various tasks.

Using Your Eyes for Communication

Eye contact in the wolf pack is one of the ways of keeping order. Only the alpha animals (male or female) use it, to remind the others of who's in charge and, in general, to maintain the status quo of the leader. To a certain extent, this is also the purpose for human-dog eye contact. When you initiate eye contact, you express your alpha position. The difference is that you don't expect your pup to turn away or avert his eyes. You will encourage your pup to maintain eye contact for several seconds, and you will make it a pleasant experience.

Use the term "watch me," or use his name to teach eye contact. You can make a noise to get his attention, wiggle your fingers up beside your eye, or move a tidbit from his nose to your eye until he understands what you want. Always praise him the instant you have eye contact — that is how he learns what you want. If you have trouble getting your pup to look at you, take his muzzle (or whole head) in your hands, and turn his head up toward you. Praise him the instant your eyes connect, then release him. A very submissive dog will have a hard time maintaining eye contact, so give him lots of encouragement. A dominant pup won't want to make eye contact on your terms, but keep working at it and praise him vigorously when he gives you even a momentary glance.

The watch me command focuses your pup's attention on you. *Photo by Jane Exon.*

Be calm and confident when you ask for eye contact. Smiling is okay. Stand up straight. You're asking for your pup's respect, so don't get down on his level for this. Read your puppy's eyes.

Continually use eye contact — in the house, on walks, whenever. The pup that grows up never having established a pattern of eye contact will become a dog that is not readily trainable, and he will have trouble learning good manners.

The watch me command teaches your pup that you want his attention — that you want him to check in with you. Therefore, it can be followed by a command such as "sit," or "this way," or it can be followed by a "good dog" and a pat on the head or shoulder. You've gotten your pup's attention — you're happy and he's happy. As you continue to get eye contact and to keep it for longer than a few seconds, you'll be delighted at your pup's expressions and at how beautiful his eyes are. That feeling seems to be mutual.

Using Your Voice for Communication

Throughout all the other aspects of puppy training, your voice is the one constant — the one prevailing influence on your puppy's basic attitude toward you. The tone of your voice can aid your puppy's blossoming sense of confidence or it can keep him watching you out of the corners of his eyes, wondering when harshness is going to strike again. The opposite of harshness is equally disturbing to a puppy but in a different way. A high-pitched baby-talk tone of voice can keep a puppy confused. He perceives that as an emotional tone, one similar to early tones of his littermates. We have seen puppy behavior settle down considerably when the owner slowed down the word flow and lowered her voice.

A growly voice when you're disciplining your pup, a happy voice when you're praising your pup, and a firm, calm voice when you're training your pup are all natural, and all make sense to your puppy. He learns to know which tone goes with which of his behaviors, and this knowledge greatly speeds the molding of his behavior. This, indeed, is puppy training.

Using the Leash for Communication

Most dog owners don't think of the leash as a means of communication. They see it as an item to prevent the pup from wandering off. But think about this. How much time will your dog, during his life, spend at the other end of the leash? Most of you probably live in communities that have a leash law. Therefore, unless you know of some open space where your dog can run loose (and we hope that you do), your dog will spend a great amount of time walking and running on a leash or on a long line (marvelous for giving the pup twenty to thirty feet of roaming and still keep him under control).

Your pup's perception of you is determined in part by the way in which he is treated on the leash. If you're rough and inconsistent with jerks and pulls, your pup will be confused. In contrast, if your pup drags you wherever he wishes, he perceives you as letting him do whatever he wants. Neither of these attitudes is a basis for good communication. Look upon your leash as a training tool. The details for doing this are described later in this chapter.

Teaching Your Puppy to Learn

Puppy training isn't obedience training. The object of puppy training is to help your pup learn how to perform certain tasks, such as sit, come, down, and walk on a leash. The tasks themselves have a purpose beyond the performance by the puppy. We use them to teach the pup *how* to learn. This means getting all of his neurons sparking in the right order so that, as he matures, he will be able to process the steps of learning and will have the commands (vocabulary) to use as building blocks in learning other activities.

What else do we mean when we say that we are teaching a puppy how to learn? We teach the pup to look at us, to listen to us, and to concentrate for a few seconds. This results in his doing the task and in his receiving praise. The watching, listening, and concentrating skills are the skills that your pup will use all of his life, and they soon will be of great value as the pup grows into adolescence and becomes more independent. If puppy kindergarten classes are available in your community, we highly recommend this experience for you and your pup.

How to Proceed

Tidbits. In the morning when you get up, put tidbits in your pocket. When you get home from work, put tidbits in your pocket. And, on days off, keep tidbits in your pocket, because you never know when you will be using one. The nice thing about puppy training is that it can be done anywhere at anytime.

Guiding your pup with tidbits to sit, to down, to come, and to walk beside you is the quickest and most stress-free way to teach your pup. The valuable part about this type of training is that it teaches your puppy to pay attention to you at the same time that it teaches him to concentrate and to focus his attention on an action. The more he does it, the more he gets praised and the more his confidence grows. A good habit is thus formed.

These tidbits should be something that your pup *really* likes, not pieces of his dog food. Oven-baked liver (baked at 350 degrees for an hour and left in the oven to dry) is always exciting to pups.

Be sure to cut the liver into very small pieces. Thinly sliced hot dogs really get a pup's attention, too. Cheese is also popular. Try popcorn with garlic powder sprinkled on it. Various commercial treats are also enticing. It's well worth the effort to find something that your pup thinks is very exciting. For the pup that isn't a chow hound, you may have to teach him to like a tidbit. At mealtime, before you show him his supper, get him excited about the tidbit that you're holding and see if he'll take it from your fingers. Toss a piece into his food bowl. All puppies can be convinced that a tidbit is a great thing — we've never seen an otherwise disinterested puppy turn down a piece of liver. The exception to using special treats is for the excitable pup that can't be readily taught to take the tidbit without turning somersaults. This pup can be trained with bits of his regular food.

We think that using tidbits is the quickest and easiest way to teach puppies how to learn. Their use, however, must be put in perspective. A tidbit is a *secondary* reward. Your voice is the *primary* reward. This means that your pup will learn that your exciting voice and playful pats are especially great because they're immediately followed by a favorite tidbit. Gradually, you will stop offering the tidbit, and then your voice and enthusiasm will become the pup's total reward.

Teaching the Tasks

Food-following is a good description for introducing the basic tasks to your puppy. You don't want to use a leash unless you are working in an area that is dangerous for an off-leash puppy. At this age, you can usually keep the pup's attention with your voice, your hands, and your body language. You want the pup to be guided into learning these tasks without the distracting pull and jerk of a leash.

Leash Training. Even though you're going to use food-following as much as possible, your pup needs to be accustomed to a leash. When you first introduce your puppy to a leash, clip it onto his collar and follow him wherever he goes. Then, with your voice and by patting your hand on your leg, encourage him to follow you for a few steps. Some pups adjust to a leash immediately, while others might need several sessions of just having

A yummy treat introduces your puppy to staying close to your side. Nancy Digby and Magic. *Photo by James Digby.*

Left: Raise the treat to your waist, but give the pup a sniff if you think he's about to be distracted. *Photo by James Digby.*

If your puppy wanders away, run backward and call him to you with "Come." *Photo by James Digby.*

the leash attached to them. The pup should wear a comfortable buckle collar — keep checking it for size because puppies grow fast. The leash should be about six feet long and made of nylon, cotton webbing, or leather. A piece of soft clothesline will also get the job done. No chain leashes, please.

The Walk Alongside. Initiate the training by using food-following. A tasty tidbit in your hand is the guide for showing your puppy that bouncing along close to your side is a great place to be. This is preferably done with no leash, but if you're in an area where you must have a leash on your puppy, fold it in your right hand until it is comfortably loose as it hangs down from the pup's collar. If you have your puppy out for a walk, do this exercise a couple of times during the walk, then let the pup whiz around, sniffing and learning about the world, the rest of the time. Use a word when you begin, such as "with me" or "let's go."

Reminders:
• Work the puppy on your left side.
• Let the pup lick and nibble the tidbit in your left hand. Talk to him and use his name. After a few training sessions, raise your hand holding the tidbit at your waist. Lower it back down in front of his nose whenever he becomes distracted. If he gets a couple of feet away from you, call him with "come." Walk backward, then give him the tidbit when he gets to you. Continue walking forward.
• Move at a pace to keep your puppy trotting or jogging.
• Stop while the pup is still paying attention to you. Gradually increase the length of time of each heeling. Begin with ten seconds.
• If your pup wanders off, you don't have his attention. Stop walking in a straight line. Try a different tidbit. Run backward and make quick turns. Give him the tidbit and begin again (or stop if he has worked long enough).
• Praise your pup at the end of each heeling "trip." Pat the pup and use a happy voice.

After your pup has done numerous food-following walks, have him walk alongside with a leash. The leash should be just long enough to hang down slightly from the pup's collar. As soon as your pup moves away from you and tightens the leash, give a slight pop on it. This should bring the pup back to your side (he wasn't very far away) and you can tell him, without slowing down, that he's a "good dog." After a minute or two of this kind of leash walking, let him relax and continue his walk with sniffing and trotting. Remember to use the release command, "okay," when you stop the short leash walking. Use the heel command now if you wish.

Checking In. Food finding is used to teach puppies to check in with their person. In the photos, the parking area is not used by cars between classes. The long line keeps the puppy from wandering off beyond a certain distance. The pup sniffs and walks around. As he comes closer, his person takes up the slack on his line but doesn't call him or use his name. As he gets closer, he becomes distracted but finally gets back to home base, a yummy treat, and lots of praise. This is repeated in different places several times.

The long line, which can be from twenty to thirty feet, should be used on walks where the pup can venture out away from you. At this point, he's familiar with checking in with you for a tidbit or praise and does so readily when you call him. Eventually, you'll reach a time and age when you can walk in an area where your dog can be off leash, and he won't just take off and run. He will be accustomed to checking in with you, with a little verbal help from you.

The retractable lead is a great help for having your dog walk out and return to you. It comes in a variety of lengths, the longest being twenty-six feet. You will enjoy the comfort and ease of using one, but it doesn't take the place of a leash. Your puppy must learn manners on a leash, because there are many areas where a leash is best.

Wait. This is a command that you will probably use more often than any other. "Wait while I open the door." "Wait while I walk out first." "Wait while I open the car door." "Wait while I

CHECKING IN

To teach your puppy to check in with you, begin by letting him explore. Do not give a come command. Gradually pull in the loose line so he won't run off if distracted. Give him lots of praise and treats when he gets back to you. Mary Marsh and Molli. *Photos by Author.*

Left: Tell your pup to wait. He can either sit or stand at this age.
Right: Be ready to correct with the leash if he starts to get ahead of you. *Photos by Scott Baily.*

go out the gate first." "Wait until that car goes by." While this command keeps your puppy from leaping and charging around, it also teaches him that you are first to do things, and then it's his turn. For many of these situations, your pup will be on a leash and you will be able to use little tugs. You can also put your hand in front of his face to remind him and block him with your leg. It takes very little time to do this consistently at every door, so don't allow yourself to be in too much of a hurry, letting your pup go charging out first. If you are consistent, your pup will learn quickly.

Place. If your pup has a mat or pad in the room where you visit with friends, watch television, etc., he can learn to go there on command and stay. This will probably take a few weeks of helping him remember what the place command means. Keep encouraging him, and use the stay command after he knows it.

Go to your "place." Every time you take your puppy to his rug or pillow, repeat "place" and give a treat. *Photo by Author.*

The Sit. Your pup is accustomed to your hand, and you'll use hand movement to teach the sit. Hold your hand with the tidbit right on top of the pup's nose. With a wiggly pup, touch the front of his nose. Say "sit" while moving your hand back (parallel to the floor, not up). As soon as he sits, say "good dog" and give him the tidbit. Don't expect him to stay there, because he's much too lively for that.

For the pup that is too bouncy to put his tail on the floor, quickly give a tidbit when the pup's hind legs bend even the slightest amount. You'll be amazed to see a good sit in two or three days. One pup took a week, but that's the exception. Continue guiding with treats until a snappy sit is consistent. As soon as your pup will sit on voice command without being guided, give him a tidbit for a job well done. Praise him first, then immediately give the tidbit. There will come a time when your praise will take the place of the tidbit.

The Come. Your hands will be the visual reinforcement of your come command. To begin teaching the command, have both hands close in front of you holding a tidbit. With your pup right there, licking the tidbit, walk backward repeating the come command. After a few steps, give the treat to the pup and praise him. A few times of doing this is usually sufficient to impress your pup with the rewards of coming right up to you.

Your come commands can be anywhere in the house or in a fenced yard. No leash is needed on the pup. Kneel down on the pup's level. Be sure that the pup is close to you, looking at you, before you tell him to come. Distance comes much later. Puppies learn quickest when they have success. Use the pup's name and then the command, "Tippy, come!" Clap your hands or pat the floor, or both. You'll find that in a month or two, when your pup is distracted by something or you're farther away, your pup will respond to your hand movements when he was initially deaf to your voice. Always use them together in the teaching phase.

Gradually increase the distance from your pup when you call him to you, but not beyond twenty to thirty feet. If he gets distracted, get his attention back on you, walking closer to him if necessary. When your pup comes all the way to you for his tidbit, touch his collar with your other hand. This helps him to be comfortable with a hand reaching for the collar in the future when you might not have a tidbit. Don't grab for the pup when he's close to you but not completely there. If you do, he'll quickly learn the play-around-just-out-of-reach game that puppies think is such fun.

A reminder (because we all tend to get frustrated at times) — *never scold your pup once he has finally come.* You needn't praise, but you simply can't show your anger, because that's a sure way to teach your pup to go the other direction when you call. Try walking away, or lie down on the ground — your pup will probably come just because you're ignoring him.

Now it's time to practice the come command in parks and open spaces. For this, you need a long line that you can buy already made, or you can go to a hardware store and make your own. Choose about thirty feet of whatever will be comfortable in your hand when your pup pulls on it. Buy a small clasp, one that isn't big and heavy, and tie it on. Another good idea is a retractable long line, called a Flexi-Lead®, available in pet-supply stores. This is the best for both you and your pup. It takes the pulling pressure off of your arms and shoulders, and your dog is always under control. Yet, it allows him the liberty of running, sniffing, and being a normal dog on a walk.

Take your pup for a walk. Let him wander around, and when he's interested in sniffing and poking around, call his name. If he doesn't look at you, call his name again and give a quick tug on the line. When he looks at you, praise him immediately and call him to you, giving him a tidbit and touching his collar. Then let him run out on his long line again. Call him to you occasionally during the walk. This teaches him to check in with you, getting a tidbit before going out again.

The Down Stay. The down command, followed by a stay (which will only be for five to ten seconds at first but gradually works up to a minute), impresses upon your pup his relationship with you — benevolent and worthy of respect. This is especially important for males or dominant breeds or individuals. For the down, put the tidbit right under your pup's nose (he's sitting), then down to the floor between his feet, and finally out in front. He should lie down as he follows it. If he doesn't, help him by *gently* pushing down on his shoulders.

After your pup has learned the down command and is comfortable with it, add the stay command. Put your foot on the leash, close to the clasp, and stand up. The pup won't be able to stand up because the leash is too short. If he wiggles, he soon finds out that he can't go anyplace, and then he lays back down again. He's teaching himself that when you say "down" and "stay," he is expected to lie down and stay there. Don't take your foot off the leash until you have released him with your voice. "Okay, good dog!"

The second step is a down stay with the leash on the floor, but you don't stand on it; therefore, you need to be ready to stop the pup the instant he starts to move. Gradually work up to a minute in time, but continue to stand close to the pup.

To teach the down stay, put your foot on the leash close to the clasp of the leash. *Photo by Jane Exon.*

When the pup starts to move, the leash reminds him to stay. *Photo by Jane Exon.*

The Sit Stay. The first step is to reach the point where your pup is comfortable sitting at your side for at least a count of five. You can stroke your pup, scratching him behind the ears to help him relax and sit still. Do not attempt this exercise before your pup is twelve weeks of age.

Some puppies are very wiggly and have to learn to sit quietly at your side before you can teach the stay. *Photo by Jane Exon.*

Fold the leash in your left hand so that it is taut, and put your hand straight up above your pup's head. Place your open right hand in front of the pup's nose. Give the command "stay." Step directly in front of your pup with your toes almost touching the pup's toes. Count to five, then step back to heel position. Count to three, release, and give praise.

A pup learns to do things in a step-by-step manner. For example, in teaching the sit stay, you must first teach him to stay while you stand toe-to-toe in front him, then to stay while you're a couple of feet in front of him. You must be able to still correct him with a tug on the leash if he starts to move. You then teach him to stay while you walk around him, and you must still be able to correct him with a tug on the leash. Then you work on the exercise while standing several feet in front of him. Many pups will take several weeks to progress through these steps, but they are necessary if you want to teach the stay effectively.

Mickie can now concentrate long enough to sit while Liz steps away. *Photo by Jane Exon.*

Puppies can learn to concentrate even with distractions for twenty to thirty seconds. *Photo by Jane Exon.*

WHAT YOU CAN EXPECT FROM YOUR PUPPY

Your training program will be in the everyday process of living with your puppy. It's *your* responsibility to insist on your pup's attention — your pup's responsibility is to be happy and playful in responding to you. To keep your pup tuned in to you, continually raise your expectations. As the weeks go by, expect the following behaviors to become consistent.

To concentrate on what he/she is doing. Begin with a few seconds of your pup's total attention while walking at your side, gradually extending the length of time up to a minute.

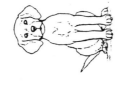

To pay attention. The Watch-Me is a good way to reinforce this (and also puts you in the alpha position.)

To look towards you when pup hears its name. Follow through with a Sit, or a Come, or just a Good Dog!

To sit. The control you have by using this command is basic to teaching your dog good manners. After you stop his/her bad behavior, insist on a "Sit." He has then responded to your authority and you praise him for good behavior.

To come when called — at a short distance off-leash, and from a farther distance on a long-line. Keep a few tidbits in your pocket to reward your pup when he gets to you.

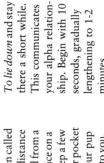

To lie down and stay there a short while. This communicates your alpha relationship. Begin with 10 seconds, gradually lengthening to 1-2 minutes.

Clicker Training

Clicker training has become popular in the dog world in recent years. It was first used about forty years ago in training dolphins and other wild animals. Karen Pryor, a renowned dolphin trainer, was among the first persons to write about this method of positive reinforcement, presenting it in vocabulary and training steps that could be used by people with their own pets. We recommend the book and video, *Karen Pryor's Clicker Training Start-up Kit* and *Clicker Magic Video*.

A variety of other books on clicker training have also been published and do a fine job of presenting the practical aspects of using a clicker. You can obtain the catalogs listed in the Bibliography for access to books on this subject. Web sites are also listed.

Clicker training is operant conditioning (positive reinforcement) where a click is paired with a reward. This motivates a dog to perform a desired physical behavior. It's not for everyone. You dog isn't on leash. You don't give any command initially, and you must watch carefully for the movement you want, clicking at the precise moment the dog is in the process of making this movement. But it's fun. You pup will love it. Give it a try.

You begin by teaching your pup the meaning of the click. Use treats that are yummy to a dog — pea-size pieces of chicken, hot dog, or hard cheese (not slices wrapped in plastic). Use a room or area that is without distractions. Don't give any commands. Stand close to you dog, click the clicker, then give the pup a treat. Repeat this four or five times and in different parts of the room or lawn. The next step is to click and delay the treat a few seconds. When the pup alerts to the sound of the clicker, you're ready to begin shaping a behavior.

Knowing a few of the basics will help you get started. Click *during* the desired movement. *The timing of the click is crucial.* You pup will stop what he's doing when he hears the click, and that's okay. The click ends the behavior. Give the treat after you click. You can lure your pup into a position or motion by using hand or body movements, but don't push, pull, or adjust with your hands. If you must have a leash on for safety reasons, loop

Left: Click and treat every time your pup's head moves toward you.
Right: He will soon make eye contact. Now you can use the watch me command and click and treat when he looks at you.
Photos by James Digby.

it in your belt. Don't let it pull or restrict the pup in any way. Keep the sessions short — no longer than five minutes.

Now choose a behavior you want to teach, such as looking at you. When your pup turns his head toward you even a little bit (make a movement if necessary), click and treat. When he raises his head slightly, click and treat. Every time he moves his head a little bit farther in the direction you want, click and treat. In your next session, review by clicking any partial movements of his head, and a bonus of several treats when he looks at you. When your pup is confident at looking at you, add the command "watch me," or whatever your command is, then click and treat. The next step is to click and treat randomly, not every time. For the sit command, perhaps you have already taught your pup by using a treat at his nose. Do that and click and treat as he sits. Wait until the pup is performing the sit without the lure of your hand before you use the sit command. Or just watch your puppy

Left: Click and treat when the back legs bend.
Right: After your pup sits regularly, give the command. Click and treat when he responds with a sit. Owner, Becky Hensen. *Photos by Author.*

for his rump to get closer to the ground before you click and treat. When he does the complete sit, you can add the command.

Karen Pryor suggests that you "catch" cute behaviors when you are with your pup, such as cocking the head or holding up a paw. You can click for a variety of different behaviors without confusing your dog. If you have two dogs, train them separately. Click for good behavior. If your pup jumps on people, don't give him any goodies unless he's sitting or has his feet on the floor. Then click and treat. If your dog barks, click and treat when he stops and is silent. When walking, click and treat when the leash is slack.

This is positive reinforcement (operant conditioning). In the traditional dog-training use of operant conditioning, the method in this book, you use your voice and treats. Clicker training uses a sound (click) and a treat. The advantage of the clicker is the timing of the click, which is very precise and tells the dog which body movement you want. The more complex the command, the more types of movement you will need to click. For this, you need a teacher or a good book and a video. Use no corrections when you are clicker training. That will disrupt the pup's attitude and perhaps lose the pup's confidence in the clicker process.

Clicker training is another avenue of communication between you and your puppy. Find out more about it and proceed to enjoy working with your puppy in a most rewarding way.

Then Versus Now in Puppy Training

The era of the small-town dog is probably gone forever. No longer does the family dog trot to the park with the kids, follow them as they move on to other pursuits, wander back home to cool off under the porch, and visit a few dog friends on the way.

No, the life of the dog is now much more formal and controlled. Because of this — because your dog no longer has the luxury of exercising his natural dog behavior, expending energy whenever his energy level is high and socializing with his own subculture of friends — you owe him a lot. You owe him as good a life as you can give him. You owe him play time and learning time so that you can live together in mutual trust, joy, and respect.

CHAPTER 12

THE SECOND SIX MONTHS

*Puppies appear to learn quickly — but then it takes a long
time for them to acquire the confidence
to perform consistently.*

There comes a day when you wonder what's wrong. Your pup
won't pay attention to you. In fact, he seems to be going out of
his way to oppose you. Well, nothing's wrong — it's just one of
the difficult times that a puppy goes through (difficult for you,
but not for him). At six or seven months of age, and again
around twelve months, your dog will challenge your leadership
in the sense that he'll ignore you. This is a very normal thing for
your pup to do, so don't get upset. Tell him that you know what
he's doing and that you're still the boss.

This is a transition age beyond puppyhood but prior to maturity. It's called adolescence, and it begins earlier in some pups and later in others. Hormones are surging during these months. If your puppy hasn't been neutered, he's becoming more intense and excitable about investigating everything in his environment. If a female hasn't been spayed, she may exhibit behaviors such as silliness and may not respond to commands that she knows. This can occur just before she comes into estrus as well as during that period of time. Being spayed or neutered will not change your dog's personality, and it will make him or her a companion that is much easier to live with.

During these months, the best approach with your pup is to keep training the basic commands and using these commands to enforce your good-behavior policy. An obedience class is an excellent idea, because it puts you on a routine with weekly goals. Your young dog will learn to respond to you even with the distraction of other dogs. But applying these commands to help your dog maintain good manners at home is up to you.

Exercise is important during this transition age. *Photo by Judith Strom.*

More Exercise, Less Freedom

Your pup will be much calmer to live with if he gets enough exercise. Play some running games. With friends or family, one person stands at the corners of an imaginary square or triangle. Each one has treats and takes turns calling your dog, waving arms to get his attention. Once he learns that everyone has a treat, he'll quickly learn to go to who is calling him. The person who has him holds the leash until he is called. If your dog runs off before he learns to go to whoever calls him, put on a long line. If the treats are yummy enough, he'll soon learn. Retrieving is another running game. Make it fun. If he doesn't return, put on a long line. Give him a treat when he gets back to you. You can stop the treat when he learns the game. Take him on short jogs, stopping or slowing fairly often.

To keep your maturing puppy from getting into destructive mischief, keep him with you or in a crate or a pen. This isn't cruel. It would be a lot more cruel if he kept destroying things and you took him to the animal shelter.

He should be with you whenever you're home. Use your leash in the house if necessary. Hopefully, he learned "place" when he was younger. If not, teach him now. He can lie beside you. This will take repetition and patience until he learns that he can't wander off. That's why you keep his leash on.

Teach him "leave it" so you have control over his grabbing and running. Put several items he's not allowed to have, as well as a cookie, etc., on the floor. When he reaches for it as you walk past, turn quickly with a brisk leash pull and say "leave it." Very soon he will walk past, ignoring the items and practically hugging your leg. You will need to repeat this periodically to reinforce "leave it."

Work diligently to teach your young dog how to behave when friends come. He is vigorous and excited, and you can't expect him to automatically be a good dog unless you teach him how to act. We can't tell you how many repetitions that will take. It depends on your consistency and your dog's level of excitability. Hopefully, you have already taught the sit command very thoroughly. If not, get busy.

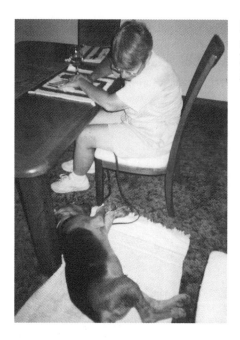

Keep your puppy with you as much as possible. Notice that Nancy is sitting on the leash. *Photo by James Digby.*

Left: Your puppy should be on leash at the door.
Right: Sometimes your puppy will need several commands before he settles down. Stay with it. The rewards are great. *Photos by James Digby.*

Do Away with a Problem by Teaching It

Is your dog still jumping on people? Teach the paws-up command, which gives him permission to do it then and only then. Does he paw you? Teach him to shake hands, alternating paws in rapid succession. Teaching your dog to do a variety of commands keeps him alert, not bored, and focuses his attention on you.

The paws up command controls a dog that insists on jumping. *Photos by the author.*

Use the Basic Commands to Control Behavior

You need an attitude of determination and a will to be consistent with your training regimen. You must insist on your dog learning good behavior when friends arrive, and on his using good door behavior when he goes in and out. You must expect your dog to respond to you and to be controlled when you're out walking and other people approach. This is where determination and consistency come in. You must insist on good behavior (without losing patience and saying, "Oh, it's hopeless"), and you must use the same procedure (consistency) each time you correct a behavior. If you can manage these two factors, you will be amazed that your dog's behavior actually does improve.

Reinforce Basic Commands

The sit command is one that you will use for control in any situation. It's an excellent way to discipline your dog in the sense that it stops his bad behavior (he can't jump or run or even bark much if he's on a sit stay), and it puts you in control and gains your dog's respect.

To make certain that your dog understands "sit" to mean "sit now," do random sits. Walk him a few steps, not on a heel command but on a "let's go," and give him the sit command. If he ignores you, put your right hand on the leash near the collar and your left hand across his back just in front of his hind legs. Pull up on the leash, and squeeze down and back with the thumb and third finger of your left hand. Repeat the "sit" as you sit him. Always be ready to use both hands to sit your dog if he doesn't respond to your command immediately. You can progress to using only the leash, tugged straight up, on the sit. Then he should begin responding to the sit without any cues from you. But *always* be ready to show him that you're alert and in control and that you will correct him instantly whenever he ignores your command.

Use this same approach when you're reviewing the other commands that your dog knows. You have to concentrate as much or more than you expect your dog to. The more you concentrate on what you're doing, the better your timing will be for a leash or a voice correction if your dog doesn't respond properly.

Insist on Good Manners

Now that your dog really understands the sit command, you can use it to teach good manners. If your dog jumps at people or at other dogs when he's out walking with you, tell him "no," give him a pop on the leash to get him back to you, and say "sit!" Let him sit there for several seconds, and get eye contact with a "watch me." At that point, you can tell him that he's a good dog and continue walking. Sometimes you will give your dog a sit command before a person gets close. Your dog can learn to sit there without leaping up until you give permission for him to move.

The sit command is excellent for teaching good manners at your front door. Some dogs are easy to teach to sit while the door is opened, but if your dog has developed a bad habit of barking and jumping and in general being out of control when someone comes to the door, you might need reinforcement of a squirt bottle with a dilute solution of vinegar and water (approximately one to six) ready to use.

Enlist some friends to help you by ringing your doorbell, then waiting patiently to enter while you work with your dog. You won't need a leash for this, because your dog will learn more quickly when he must be totally responsible for his own actions without being tugged and pulled on a leash.

When your dog becomes very excited and is barking at the door, give a sit command. He will probably keep barking because he's so excited. Repeat the sit command, and squirt at his lips with the vinegar water. Keep repeating the sit command and the squirt until your dog sits. You might be several feet away from the door by now because your dog will keep moving around, but just keep moving with him. When he is finally sitting and not barking, calmly and quietly tell him that he's a good dog. After your friends come through the door, you can release your dog from his sit. If he wants to jump up, insist that he sit again. Use the squirt bottle if necessary. Once you and your dog understand this procedure at the door, the dog will be more relaxed (as will you) and will sit without all the jumping around, and without being squirted with vinegar water. Nevertheless, keep a bottle near the door for reinforcement.

The sit stay reminds your dog to wait until given another command. *Photo by Jane Exon.*

Take advantage of any distractions to keep training your adolescent dog on a sit stay. *Photo by Jane Exon.*

Another good use of the sit command is to have your dog wait while you open the door. You will step out the door, then call your dog to you. The same procedure applies when you come back in. This reminds him of who's in control, and it keeps him from bolting out the door or knocking you over to be the first one into the house.

The sit command can also be used if your dog is playing around out of reach and won't come to you. Keep saying "sit-sit-sit," pointing your finger and staring at him. Follow him wherever he wiggles or moves to, and you *will* get a sit from him. Now go to him and tell him that he's a good dog because he sat. This procedure reinforces the come command when your dog is feeling his independence.

The Come

A long line is essential now so that you are in control and can make your dog come to you even if he doesn't want to. After several weeks of using a long line or Flexi-Lead® and rewarding him for coming and checking in with you, your dog should be reliable off leash in safe fields or greenbelt areas. One of our students, Jim, was considering renting an electronic collar because his Standard Schnauzer needed exercise but kept running off. We discussed the pros and cons; two weeks later he phoned and said that he didn't need the remote-control collar — cheese had done the job. Keep calling your dog to you, give a reward, and let him run off again — but don't let him get too far away before calling him.

The Down Stay

Practice this when you want your dog in the room with you, such as at mealtime, but not moving around being a nuisance. With a leash attached to your dog's collar, put him on a down stay (which he has learned previously). If he gets up, give him a correction. Put him down by giving a brisk pop down on the leash. Look him straight in the eye and repeat "down, stay!" If he gets up one more time, tie his leash to a heavy piece of furniture or other stable item so that when he tries to stand up, he won't be able to. This also increases his respect for you. "Down stay" means to lie down and stay there, with no exceptions.

Walking on the Leash

When you walk your dog in a park, or any public area. respect the other people who also use the park. Take some plastic sandwich bags with you. When your dog defecates, put a plastic bag on your hand like a mitten, pick up the feces, and pull the bag off so that the pile you picked up is now inside the bag. Carry a small paper bag with you to keep the plastic bag in until you reach a garbage container. If dog owners would do this, they would be more welcome in public areas.

Use the come command when your dog is pulling too hard on the leash. Call your dog, walk backward a few steps, and reward him when he gets to you. Now walk forward again and let him move along beside you. Repeat calling him to you whenever he pulls on the leash. Using a Flexi-Lead® takes a lot of pressure off your arms and shoulders and gives the dog more freedom and distance to exercise.

Behavioral Traits

Your pup's personality will continue to develop during the next few months. The drives we discussed in Chapter 1 are now beginning to show and can cause distractions for the dog at times. For example, a retriever will run off and chase a bird even if there is no chance he can catch it. Some behavioral traits don't become strongly developed until the dog is a year old or more. Traits such as stubbornness and extreme independence were undoubtedly hinted at during puppyhood but were very easy to ignore because "he was only a puppy," or because it hadn't become a problem yet. With puppy training, you have likely nipped many problems before they have become deeply entrenched. As the dog matures, however, you must continue to assert your role of leadership.

Other behavioral problems, such as barking or a lapse in housetraining, can be caused by stress or by a change in the daily home routine. Such stresses might include a stay in a boarding kennel or a schedule change by a member of the family who had previously been at home and then went back to school or work.

Every time your dog starts to drag you on the leash, call him by name to come to you. *Photos by Jane Exon.*

Some behavioral traits aren't very noticeable until the dog reaches sexual maturity, and then they can become obvious problems requiring attention. Roaming and overprotectiveness are some examples. The roaming dog must not have the opportunity to wander. He must be confined in a yard or house, or be under your total control when he's outside of his home.

Some dogs have a genetic disposition toward protectiveness, and sexual maturity accentuates it. Some dogs will just naturally try an aggressive reaction in certain circumstances, and when they find out that you won't permit it, they cease that type of behavior. When you are walking your dog on leash, any demonstration of growling or lip curling must immediately be stopped. An instant "NO," accompanied by an abrupt turn in the opposite direction for a few steps, then followed by a "sit" and a "watch me" should work. Tell him that you won't permit such behavior. You can now turn back to where you were. If he behaves, tell him that he's a good dog.

Territoriality

Almost all dogs have a sense of territory. Unless a dog has been totally forbidden to do so, he will automatically announce the arrival of someone at the door or on the property. Some dogs have stronger-than-average senses of territory and enlarge their area to include the route of their regular walks through the neighborhood. An aggressive male dog could become a problem because of trying to fight other males that are intruding on his street or sidewalk. The degree of a dog's protective actions is based on the relationship that you have established with him. If you have let him have his own way, the protectiveness will begin to show at this age. The pup will begin to put himself in the role of pack leader. This means that if he has tendencies toward overprotectiveness, he will begin to become aggressive if someone comes near his food bowl, or to growl at your friends.

Some people think that they want a guard dog and should allow this kind of behavior. This is not correct. It isn't necessary to encourage aggressive actions in order to have a dog that barks and warns you of strangers. Most dogs will automatically do this. A dog that is not controllable is dangerous to have around. Now is the time to get involved with a formal training program and get your relationship back on track.

Separation Anxiety

This is defined as dogs who engage in disruptive behaviors when left home alone, such as barking, howling, chewing, digging, and elimination. It's not disobedience. It's a dog in distress, a dog that is well-behaved when you're home but becomes intensely stressed when you leave. You might have taught your pup to stay home alone as discussed on p. 109, but now, several months later, the problem arises and you wonder what you can do about it. Punishment is not effective and is inappropriate. You cannot put your dog in a crate when dealing with separation anxiety. It only intensifies his anxiety to the extent of damaging the crate or breaking out through its door.

Most anxiety behaviors occur during the first five to ten minutes after you leave home. There are several things you can do to help your dog relax during this time. One of these is to practice graduated departures, perhaps taking a weekend to work on this. Some dogs begin their stress behaviors instantly, so start by timing your absence for just a few seconds and then return. We've had dogs where we began by closing the door and opening it again. Work up to a minute, then two minutes, back to one minute, then three. Work up to five minutes, and when your dog appears calm at your return, begin to work for longer times, periodically going back to two or three minutes.

Use the same cue words each time you leave, such as, "See you soon. Be a good dog." It doesn't matter what words you say as long as they're always the same and spoken in a neutral voice. Each time you depart, give your dog a chew toy that is stuffed with biscuits, and a hollow, sterilized bone with some cheese in it. These will keep your pup busy for the first few minutes. If you've been leaving the radio on during your absence, change to using the television.

Think about your actions just before you leave the house. Practice your routine, leave, then return right away. You can do this several times during a day but not during the timed departures. For example, put your coat on, reach for your purse or car keys and whatever else you do, and then leave. Your goal is to eliminate stress when your dog watches these activities by making it a common event after which you return.

If these routines aren't changing the behavior, seek professional help. Most veterinarians are familiar with this problem and will know if there is a medication that will help your dog deal with the initial anxiety. Then you can begin again with the procedures discussed above.

Communication

You talk to your dog, and he responds to many words that you use. Dogs learn a vocabulary of 100 words or more. They know the meaning of outside, walk, supper, car, cookie, sit, stay, and others. Unfortunately, you become so intent on what you want to say to your dog that you forget to listen to what your dog has to say to you. Words don't exist in the dog world, but communication with them is still possible and indispensable.

Dogs use signals. This includes all parts of their body, but especially the head and eyes, the lips, the ears, the eyebrows, and various wrinkles. Even though you delight in watching your dog and playing with him as he matures, you don't see most of these signals because you don't know about them, or you don't understand their meaning. Sometimes a dog signals so quickly that you miss it. One of these signals is lip licking.

I thought that Mitzi, the Dachshund who came to live with us at age seven, didn't use licking signals until a friend came to visit and knelt on the floor, stroking and greeting her. I watched as the tip of Mitzi's tongue responded with lip licking. Now I know that when someone greets her at her level, she has the pleasure of returning the greeting.

Lip licking isn't always a greeting. Sometimes it's used for a calming effect. Have you spoken sharply to your dog? Or are you not feeling well? You might see your dog approach with lip licking. Talk to your dog and acknowledge his signal. If this excites him, tell him about that, too. He won't understand your words, but he will sense your intent.

Have you had the wonderful experience of catching a look of surprise or a startled expression on your dog? (They're similar but not identical.) The eyes get big — you know exactly what's being communicated by the shape of the mouth and facial muscles. But these are fleeting signals. If you aren't aware, you'll miss them.

The yawn is an example of one that is not quickly gone. You can't miss it. With the dog, it can be an expression of insecurity, embarrassment, or relief. It can also be used to show friendliness between dogs, such as a dominant dog to a submissive one. One place you might see a yawn is during a training session — for example, when you are teaching the stay or the heel command, and your intensity or nervousness causes your dog to feel insecure. When you relax and use a more pleasant voice, and your dog becomes confident of what you want from him, the need for a yawn disappears.

Lip licking and yawning can have any one of several meanings, so how do you know which one your dog is communicating? Think about the context of the signal — what you are doing, what is going on at that moment. The more you observe your dog's signals, the better you will understand them, and the better you will know your dog. If you are interested in learning more about dog signals, read the book *On Talking Terms with Dogs: Calming Signals* by Turid Rugaas. See the Bibliography for ordering information.

Sexual Maturity

The indication that the female has reached sexual maturity is the onset of estrus, commonly called the heat period. This is not an indication of physical or behavioral maturity, because there is still much growth yet to occur in these areas. There is an apparent correlation between breed size and the onset of the first estrus. It generally occurs at six to eight months for females less than thirty pounds, at eight to ten months for females thirty to sixty pounds, and at ten to fifteen months for breeds greater than sixty pounds. However, there are always individual differences in these age groups. The total length of the heat period lasts about three weeks.

The male, at some time during the last half of the first year, will begin to lift his leg to urinate. This is usually viewed as a mark of the sexually maturing male and can begin anywhere from five to twelve months, or even later. Sexual maturity often brings on an increased attitude of protectiveness and an intense interest in other dogs. As we have already stated, you may have to take specific steps to reinforce your position as pack leader.

After the male reaches the age where he is leg-lifting, he might begin to do it to excess. Leg-lifting is the manner in which a male marks his territory. Many people think that they must allow their dog to stop at every blade of grass if that is what the dog wants. Excessive leg-lifting is often a demonstration that the dog has a strong tendency toward being the pack leader, and this is one way of telling you that he's taking over the job. In small breeds, this often occurs in the house. Leg-lifting to such an excess isn't necessary. It isn't pleasant to take a dog for a walk if he's constantly stopping to lift his leg. Therefore, during your walk, have a couple of stops where he can lift his leg several times. Then continue the walk at a brisk pace on your terms. The routine can be adjusted to fit the involved individuals as long as the dog gets his bladder empty and as long as you remain in charge.

Undesirable Behaviors

This is the age when young males begin to display behaviors that you might find very objectionable. Male hormones surge to a peak of nine times normal and then level back down again, which is one reason why this is a period of behavioral changes. Some males go through a phase of continually trying to mount other dogs. This is part of the maturing process and is in the category of play and trying new behavioral activities (which doesn't mean that you have to allow it to go on and on). Distraction is sufficient discipline for most dogs. If your young male has exceptional qualities and is being considered for breeding stock, it's best not to severely discipline the dog, because this could affect his breeding desire in the future. When your dog begins to mount another dog, call him to you, or use your leash or your hand on his collar to move him away. Then you can distract him, praise his attention to you, and give him a sit command with a piece of biscuit for a reward. (Don't you always have a few biscuits in your pocket when you take a walk, or even just around the house?)

Another disturbing behavior is when your dog mounts a person's leg or any other object to which the dog takes a fancy. Use the off command for your correction. Insist that the dog stop by using his collar and scruff for a quick shake as you pull him away. Then give him a sit command and praise him when he obeys your command and his attention is on you.

With consistent correction, followed by a command such as "sit" (which is a behavior that you can praise), many dogs will keep these behaviors to a minimum. For the dog that continues to be extreme in mounting other dogs, or persons' legs, the solution is either to neuter the dog or to remove the dog from the stimulus of people or other dogs when he can't otherwise be controlled. A drug treatment is available, and your veterinarian can be consulted about this, as well as about the potential side effects.

Some males have the irritating habit of lifting their leg in the house, often in one particular room or on certain pieces of furniture. The smaller breeds seem to be more persistent in this activity than the large breeds. If your dog has a favorite area, keep it cleaned and deodorized. Dogs will naturally mark a spot that has been used previously. Another possible reason for this behavior is that your dog considers the house to be his territory (you just happen to live there and provide food). An obedience course can help you and your dog understand your relationship with each other. If your dog persists in this behavior, neutering is recommended.

Spaying and Neutering

One of the ways in which dogs can be helped to adjust to an urban or suburban environment is to spay or neuter them. This is *not* mistreating the dog or depriving him of natural feelings that are his "right." If the hormones don't send the message to the brain, the dog doesn't know what he's missing. In fact, it makes his life more pleasant because it removes some of the behavioral traits with which people find it difficult to live.

Don't consider keeping your male or female for breeding unless he or she is an outstanding individual in the breed and you are willing to spend all the time necessary to learn what must be learned before you can become a conscientious breeder. In addition, be willing to volunteer your time and effort to work in your community with the pet overpopulation problem. Many breeds have rescue projects that take a dog of their breed out of the shelter, do any training that needs doing, then find it a home.

The Female. There is no reason for your female to have one heat period before she is spayed. If you would like to avoid the problem of confining her while she's in heat, try to time the operation before her first heat period. If she isn't spayed until after her heat period, it's a good idea to wait for about two months, because it takes this long for the progesterone level to decline completely. If progesterone secretion is suddenly stopped, nervousness or irritability may occur for a time. This can be offset, however, by having your veterinarian administer a long-acting progestin. The behavior of the bitch remains normal after the spay operation, because this is the natural condition of the female between heat periods. A common myth about spaying is that the bitch becomes fat and lazy. If these should occur, it's a result of overfeeding and under-exercising.

The Male. Neutering or castration does not change the dog's masculine appearance, because he will still acquire his secondary sex characteristics regardless of his age when the procedure is done. A study conducted by Dr. Benjamin Hart and reported in his book, *Canine Behavior*, indicates that castration doesn't affect hunting ability or watch-dog behavior. There are individual differences in how it affects other behaviors. Some differences are probably a result of the environment, but many are due to breed and genetics. Roaming showed the greatest degree of change, with more than 90 percent of the dogs having either a

Well-socialized dogs are a joy to take walking. These two are six and eleven months old. *Photo by Jane Exon.*

rapid or gradual decline. This is probably a result of the lessening in sexual drive. Fighting with other male dogs showed 40 percent to have a rapid decline and 22 percent a gradual decline. About 50 percent showed a decline in urine-marking in the house. The act of mounting dropped rapidly in about one-third of the dogs studied and gradually declined in another one-third. Much of this decline was in mounting people so that castration appeared to be a good way to reduce this problem.

There doesn't appear to be any proven difference in effect from castration before puberty or in the adult dog. In fact, some humane shelters and some breeders are neutering their pups by four months of age before they are placed in their new homes. Recent studies have shown no ill effects. And as is true with the female spay operation, there is no basis for the idea that castrated dogs become fat and lazy.

This is Aspen with Paige on Aspen's first birthday. She's learned much, and her family is looking forward to a happy, lively year ahead.

The Canine Good Citizen Test

This is a goal worth working toward as you continue to train and socialize your growing puppy. We've seen seven- and eight-month-old pups pass the test, but even if the two of you might not be ready by your pup's first birthday, you will be surprised how soon it will come about, and you will be delighted with the handsome certificate. This is a low-stress test, usually offered in city parks by the various dog clubs of the area.

To receive certification as a Canine Good Citizen, a dog must pass a ten-step test. Passing the test confirms that a dog has the training and attitude to behave in a mannerly fashion at home, in public places, and in the presence of other dogs. A dog of any breed can do this. The test requires a dog to calmly allow a stranger (the test giver) to approach his handler; to show no sign of resentment or shyness while being petted by the stranger; to permit the stranger to brush or comb the dog, and to examine his ears and feet. The dog must heel on a loose lead (on either side of the handler), as well as demonstrate that he can move politely through a group of three or four people. The dog must sit or down and stay on command, and come when called.

The dog must show no more than a casual interest when another handler with a dog approaches, shakes, and talks with the dog's owner. Although the dog may express natural curiosity or even appear slightly startled, he should accept, without panic or anger, distracting situations such as something noisy being dropped or a jogger running by. If a dog begins to get excited, he must settle down when his handler speaks to him. The final test demonstrates the dog's ability to stay on leash in the company of a stranger for three minutes while his owner is out of sight. Mild agitation is acceptable, but the dog must not whine, bark, or pace unnecessarily. For more information about the Canine Good Citizen® program, contact the AKC's Director of Operations for CGC, Nancy Matlock, at (919) 854-0159.

You and your dog can earn this certificate. Insist on good manners at home. The sit and down commands are good for this. Insist on good manners when you're out walking, meeting other people and dogs, and this will all come about. Receiving that certificate will give you a mighty good feeling and is a milestone for you and your dog in working as a team.

Don't Worry — Have Fun!

During much of this chapter, we've been looking at worst-case scenarios. We certainly don't want to leave you with a dismal attitude concerning this age span of your pup's growth. It's a fun age, and our point is that many bad behaviors can be squelched immediately if you get at them as soon as they occur. If we didn't think that the rewards would be vastly greater than your training efforts, we wouldn't have written the book. Good luck — and let us know how things turn out.

The Canine Good Citizen Test is a goal worth working toward. *Photo by Judith Strom.*

AFTERWORD

You've brought your puppy a long way and have developed a good communication system. Now you can look forward to a long and satisfying relationship which sometimes will take more effort than you care to spend and at other times will have more rewards than you had dared to hope for.

If you have helped your puppy to become a good family member, then you have in a small but nonetheless significant way contributed to helping the dog become a better and consequently more acceptable part of modern society. In this event, we would like to congratulate and thank you for joining the ranks of dog lovers in our combined effort to foster good interaction between man and dog, thereby enriching all our lives. If we had a much higher proportion of well-cared-for, well-behaved animals and less of the wandering garbage hounds, the dog's image with the growing army of the urban and rural disgruntled might not be so bad.

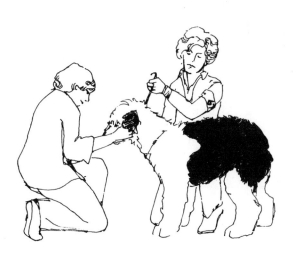

APPENDIX
Puppy Temperament Training

Author's Note

To put puppy testing in proper perspective, it is important to note that it is *one* of the tools to use in evaluating a puppy's temperament. The other tools are the breeder's continuing observation of each puppy's behavior throughout the first seven weeks, not only in the litter but also when separated and spending time with a person, and a knowledge of the behavioral factors in that particular breed and in those particular bloodlines. The puppy buyer should not get hung up on the scoring but realize it's an indication of the pup's socialization needs in the pup's new home. Dominance, shyness, and overexcitability are readily identifiable and are general traits that need special placement in homes that are willing to work with these personalities.

Many of you might select your puppy without using the test we have here. We discuss this type of puppy selection in Chapter 1 on page 7 and give you steps to help you evaluate the personalities of the puppies from which you are choosing.

The Temperament Test

Whether you use the more general selection process or the puppy temperament test that follows, the most important personality traits you will evaluate are willingness to please and willingness to forgive. Willingness to please is noted in the Coming, the Following, and the Retrieving tests. Willingness to forgive is shown in the Restraint, the Pinch test, and Social Dominance.

It's easy and fun to administer puppy tests, but it's also easy to form snap judgments as a result of the tests. A puppy test is an *indication* of the puppy's natural attitude toward people and a relative measure of the pup's submissiveness and aggressiveness. As such, it's a guide to what type of home and what kind of training will work best. It's *not* a permanent labeling of the pup's adult personality. One reason for this is that environment plays such a large part in the development of a dog's personality.

William Campbell was one of the first to develop this series of puppy tests, which give a consistent overall picture of a puppy's basic emotional behavior. Wendy Volhard and Gail Tamases Fisher have contributed greatly to the widespread use of what they term puppy aptitude testing. Our score sheet is modeled after theirs and lists the reactions we have found to be fairly common. The analysis sheet is a guide to interpreting the results of the testing and incorporates our interpretations of scoring based on observations of the testing we have done.

Breeders who use puppy testing tend to develop a sharp eye from experience. They become familiar with the behavioral tendencies of their bloodlines and with how certain reactions will develop later in adult dogs. They also can see certain behavioral qualities that are not testable, such as that extra spark of smarts or charisma. Some puppies will have a reaction not listed on the score sheet. A pup will not be shy but will be content to observe and quietly do what is indicated, but in his own time. This is probably an indication of a slightly more than average independence, or possibly an easygoing, quiet disposition. The pup can be retested another day to make certain he wasn't tired at the first test.

Many breeders prefer to conduct the test by scoring each pup in the litter while another person does the actual testing. This gives the breeder an overall view of the behavior of the litter, and this information can be helpful when discussing selection with potential new owners. The breeder might be surprised to discover that a puppy's test score can be quite different from what his litter behavior indicated. A puppy that is very quiet, even to the extent of being picked on by the others, can score as an outgoing, people-oriented pup. The reverse can also be true. An assertive pup in the litter might hesitate in association with a new person. Observation of the litter behavior with the other pups can sometimes give a false impression of the pup's innate desire to please and to adjust to people, so it's always advisable for a breeder to puppy-test a litter even though it sometimes might seem unnecessary.

Guidelines for Testing

Seven weeks of age is the optimum age for testing. The pup has the brain waves of an adult dog but is not affected to any degree by experience and learning. Therefore, the tests reveal the puppy's basic individual temperament. The object is to test each puppy in the same environment and at the same level of activity. The tests should be administered by a person unknown to the pups and conducted in a room or area that is new to them. These two factors are the means of introducing a puppy's reaction to a new person and a new environment into the testing. The place of the testing should be away from the noise of the litter and with as few distractions as possible. The time of the testing should be during one of the play times in their daily schedule, but not immediately after mealtime. If any of the pups fall asleep, give them time to run around and wake up first. Each pup, when taken from the litter, should be given a couple of minutes to urinate or defecate before being taken to the tester. During each of the test activities, the tester can use voice and hand motions.

Performing the Tests

Come. The breeder or helper carries the pup and places him on the floor or grass four feet in front of the kneeling tester. He stands for a second, then leaves. (If the puppy follows the helper, he is placed again.) As soon as the pup is on the floor, the tester gets the pup's attention using a soft voice and hands and patting the floor if necessary. The tester strokes the pup a few seconds and the observer notes the actions of the puppy — jumping on tester, climbing on lap, grabbing the sweater, running off, or quietly accepting the stroking. If the pup doesn't come, the tester reaches out with his hand, wiggling his fingers and quietly coaxing the pup. You want the pup to experience success, but the scoring will be a no-come.

Following. The tester slowly stands close to the puppy, encouraging the pup with his voice and by hand patting his leg, to follow. The pup might jump and run alongside, getting in the way, or walk with his tail down, or leave and go somewhere else. Staying at your side for two or three steps constitutes a following.

Restraint. This test is immediately followed by the Forgiveness test. For the restraint, the tester, kneeling, gently rolls the pup over on his back, keeping one hand on the puppy's chest. The pressure is just enough to keep the pup from getting up. The tester maintains a neutral, pleasant expression for thirty seconds, with no talking, and notices if the pup gives him any eye contact. This test and the Forgiveness test are the most important ones for evaluating the type of home that is best for the puppy. The best pup for the average home is the pup that shows little dominance and that reacts without fear (middle range).

Forgiveness. As soon as the pup is on his feet, the tester sits him at a forty-five-degree angle in front, using an arm or hand for a second to keep him in place. Then the tester strokes from head to tail, leaning down so that his face is available to be licked. The tester can talk to the pup. The unforgiving puppy will turn his head away. This pup will mature into a dog that will hold a grudge or will refuse to respond if the owner does something he doesn't like. The forgiving pup will wash the face or gently lick or nuzzle the cheek with his nose. The independent pup will walk away. The aggressive pup will growl or nip the tester.

Above: Some pups need encouragement to get them started on the social attraction test. *Below:* This pup decides to catch up. Two or three steps can be considered a follow. *Photos by Author.*

Use just enough pressure on the puppy to keep him on his back when he wiggles. Note if you get any eye contact. *Photo by James Digby.*

Does the puppy forgive after being restrained or toe pinched? Give him an opportunity to lick your cheek. *Photo by James Digby.*

Elevation Dominance. This test shows the degree of accepting human dominance when the pup has no control over the situation. The tester laces his fingers under the pup and lifts until the pup's feet are several inches off the floor. This position is maintained for thirty seconds with no talking. The relaxed pup that just hangs there will, as an adult, accept conditions over which he has no control. The dominant puppy won't accept this position without a struggle. The shy pup will freeze — this is a puppy that will have trouble adapting to new situations.

Retrieving. Retrieving a sheet of typing paper crumpled up into a ball is an indication of concentration and desire to please. This test is applicable to all breeds. It's more of a test of willingness to perform a task than of retrieving. The tester gets the pup's attention by touching his lips and teasing him with it. The ball is tossed about three feet away. If he goes out to it, he demonstrates he can pay attention to an object. If he brings it back to you, he has a strong desire to please or to work with a person. Some puppies, even retrieving breeds, aren't interested in going out to the tossed paper ball. This isn't a mark against them. Retrieving is a game you can teach later. Look for the pup's willingness to please in other areas of the testing.

Touch Sensitivity. This tests the pup's sensitivity to pain. The tester either sits the pup beside him or holds him in the crook of the arm. He then takes a front foot and puts pressure between the toes with the thumb and index finger. Squeezing with increasing pressure, the tester counts from one to ten. The pressure stops as soon as the puppy reacts, either by jerking the foot or biting or yipping: the overly sensitive puppy that can't deal with the light pressure of the first or second count. The middle range indicates a dog that will respond readily to collar and leash training. The pup whose count is in the top of the range isn't touch sensitive, and training will likely take more time and effort.

Sound Sensitivity. This test shows the puppy's reaction to a loud sound. When the pup faces away, the tester hits a metal pan with a spoon. The pup that notices the sound, locates it, and perhaps walks toward it is very confident. The pup that startles and

Support the puppy so that he feels secure.
Photo by James Digby.

After you get the pup's attention on the crumpled ball, toss it about four feet. The string is optional.
Photo by James Digby.

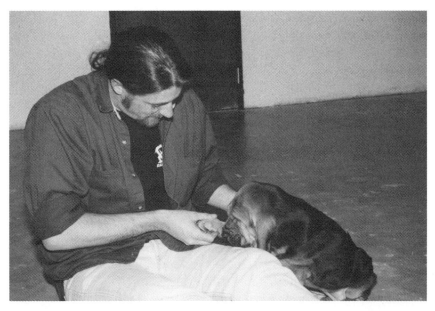

The large puppy can sit beside you for the toe pinch. This is followed by lowering your face for a forgiving kiss. *Photo by James Digby.*

recovers quickly is a very normal pup. The pup that runs away and tries to hide is very sound sensitive and shouldn't be placed in a noisy family or with someone who will be taking him to dog events or other events that are noisy. If the pup has no reaction, try again. This might be an independent puppy or possibly one that is deaf if you have a breed in which this occurs.

Sight Sensitivity. This test allows the puppy to interact with a new object. Playful interaction shows adaptability to new situations. The pup that cowers or startles will have a tough time in new situations.

Energy Level. This category is another aid in matching the puppy to the prospective owner. The high-energy person won't be happy with a quiet puppy, and the person whose life-style is calm and whose exercise consists of a walk around the block won't be able to deal with a puppy that is always in motion.

Notes and Observations

Notes can be as important as the test scores. We can attest to the vital role of note taking. One prospective puppy owner was looking for an assertive pup that could take a lot of work and training but that also had a strong desire to please. She had the first pick of the litter and had narrowed the selection to two puppies with similar scores on the puppy test. However, her notes told her that Puppy One had come to the tester on the first Come test even though he was distracted by a frayed rug corner. Puppy Two needed three comes. Early records by the breeder showed that Puppy One was the only puppy that didn't cry when removed from the litter and put on a cement floor at three and a half weeks of age. He also was the most investigative pup with a rapidly wagging tail. This cinched the selection, but she needed the written notes to help her with her decision.

The puppy-testing session is an excellent opportunity for making general observations under conditions that are the same for all the puppies. What is each pup's reaction to the tester and to the surroundings? Is he generally very curious and active, or is he hesitant? Does he whine? Write down all the observations. It's amazing how easy it is to forget the little details when observing several puppies.

For the potential owner, the breeder can point out the more cautious pups from the more aggressive ones and can also casually incorporate the Come and the Follow tests into the visit. In the final analysis, the selection of a puppy is probably more emotional than logical. However, it's best to place the pup in the home that fits his natural personality. Many future problems can be prevented this way. An assertive person will quickly lose patience with a quiet puppy, and a shy person will never be able to become the leader of a puppy with a dominant personality.

Puppy ID _____   Litter _____   Tester _____

Date _____   Age of Litter _____   Note Taker _____

Test	Description	Response	#
SOCIAL ATTRACTION Place puppy in test area. From a few feet away the tester coaxes the pup to come by clapping hands gently and kneeling down. Tester must coax in a direction away from the point where the puppy entered the testing area.	Degree of social attraction, confidence or dependence.	Came readily, tail up, jumped, barked, bit at hands.	1
		Came readily, tail up, pawed, licked at hands.	2
		Came readily, tail up.	3
		Came readily, tail down	4
		Came hesitantly or no come, fearful	5
		Did not come at all. Wanders and sniffs.	6
FOLLOWING Tester stands up and walks away from the pup in a normal manner. Make sure the pup sees tester walk away.	Degree of following attraction. Not following indicates independence or fear.	Followed readily, tail up, got underfoot, bit at feet.	1
		Followed readily, got underfoot.	2
		Followed readily, tail up.	3
		Followed readily, tail down.	4
		Huddles, won't move	5
		No follow or went away.	6
RESTRAINT Tester on hands and knees. Gently roll pup onto back and hold with one hand for a full 30 seconds.	Degree of dominant or submissive tendency. How puppy accepts stress when socially/physically dominated.	Struggled fiercely, flailed, bit.	1
		Vigorously flailed, some eye contact.	2
		Settled, struggled, settled with good eye contact.	3
		Struggled, then settled with some eye contact.	4
		No struggle - freezes	5
		No struggle, strained to avoid eye contact.	6
SOCIAL DOMINANCE Tester is still kneeling. Sit pup across your front, slightly facing you. Give him a few seconds to settle down then gently stroke him from the head to the back. Continue stroking until a recognizable behavior is established.	Degree of acceptance of social dominance. Pup may try to dominate by jumping & nipping or may be independent and walk away.	Jumped, pawed, bit, growled.	1
		Jumped, pawed.	2
		Cuddles up to tester, licks face.	3
		Squirms, licks hands.	4
		Rolls over, huddles	5
		Went away and stayed away	6

Test	Purpose	Response	Score
ELEVATION DOMINANCE Tester still kneeling. Pick up pup, cradle pup under its belly, fingers interlaced, palms up, and elevate pup to just off the ground. Hold there for 30 seconds.	Degree of accepting dominance while in a position of no control.	Struggled fiercely, bit, growled.	1
		Settled then struggled.	2
		No struggle, relaxed.	3
		Struggled, then settled.	4
		No struggle, froze.	5
		No struggle, no eye contact.	6
RETRIEVING Kneel beside pup and attract his attention with crumpled paper. When pup shows interest and is watching, toss the object 3 feet in front of pup.	Degree of willingness to work with a human. High correlation between ability to retrieve and successful guide dogs, obedience dogs, field trial dogs.	Chases object, picks up and runs away.	1
		Chases object and does not return.	2
		Chases object, returns with it to tester.	3
		Chases object and returns to tester without it.	4
		Stays with tester, worried	5
		Does not chase object.	6
TOUCH SENSITIVITY Take webbing of a front foot between your finger and thumb. Press lightly then increasingly firmly until you get a response while you slowly count to 10. Stop as soon as puppy pulls away. Repeat with ear.	Degree of sensitivity to touch.	8-10 counts before response.	Note # Counts
		6-7 counts before response.	Toe ____
		5-6 counts before response.	
		2-4 counts before response.	Ear ____
		1-2 counts before response.	
2ND SOCIAL DOMINANCE Continue holding pup in your arms until he either forgives by licking your cheek or struggles to get down.	Degree of forgiveness.	Pup quickly forgives and licks.	⬅ Circle 1
		Slow or no forgiving	

SOUND SENSITIVITY Place pup in center of area. Strike pan with a large spoon a few feet behind the puppy. Repeat.	Degree of sensitivity to sound. May be a rudimentary test for deafness.	Listens, locates sound, walks toward it barking. 1 Listens, locates sound, shows curiosity and walks toward it. 2 Listens, locates sound 3 Listens, startles 4 Cringes, backs off, hides. 5 Ignores sound, shows no curiosity. 6
SIGHT SENSITIVITY Place pup in center of area. Jerk a towel, tied to a string, across the floor a few feet from the puppy.	Degree of intelligent response to a strange object.	Looks, attacks, bites. 1 Looks, grabs, head shaking. 2 Looks curiously, plays. 3 Looks, tail tuck. 4 Runs away, hides. 5 Ignores it, no interest. 6
ENERGY LEVEL Note how active pup is throughout the testing	☐ Jumps up all the time (boing-boing) ☐ Happy and bouncy ☐ Happy, relaxed	☐ Slow, Quiet ☐ Little Participation (The Observer) ☐ No Interest

ANALYSIS OF PUPPY TEST

1. Mostly "5" responses. Shies away for no reason. Retest to verify. This pup needs a low-stress environment.

2. Mostly "4" responses. A submissive but not shy puppy. Needs confidence building. Very trainable if not rushed. Easy to live with.

3. Mostly "3" responses, with some "4s." Will be a happy dog. Good with children. Good for the inexperienced trainer. A family companion.

4. Mostly "3" responses, with some "2s." Will fit in a family with older children. Very active and does best with obedience training.

5. Mostly "2" responses, with some "3s." Outgoing and eager to please but needs a firm hand or will make a pest of himself.

6. Mostly "2" responses. Learns quickly and needs firm, consistent training. Does best with a person who has had training experience.

7. Mostly "1" responses. Very dominant. Not good with children. Untrustworthy around strangers. Needs special training with very experienced, dominant trainer. Can easily become aggressive.

8. Mostly "6" responses. Three "6s" in the first five tests is a very independent puppy. Doesn't require a lot of human attention. Training requires much repetition and patience.

BIBLIOGRAPHY

Bataglia, Carmen L., "Developing High Achievers," *AKC Gazette* 5 (1995): 47–50.

Fisher, Gail T., "A Click Away," *AKC Gazette* 9 (1998): 48–51.

Fisher, Gail T. and Wendy Volhard, "Puppy Personality Profile," *AKC Gazette* 3 (1985): 36–42.

Fogle, Bruce. *The Dog's Mind.* New York: Howell Book House, 1992.

Pryor, Karen. *A Dog and a Dolphin 2.0, An Introduction to Clicker Training.* North Bend, Washington: Sunshine Books, 1996.

Rugaas, Turid. *On Talking Terms with Dogs: Calming Signals.* Kula, Hawaii: Legacy by Mail, Inc., 1997.

SOURCES OF INFORMATION

"Dog and Cat Book Catalog." P.O. Box 2778, Wenatchee, WA 98801. Phone: 800-776-2665. www.dogandcatbooks.com

"J and J Dog Supplies." P.O. Box 1517, Galesburg, IL 61402-1517. Phone: 800-642-2050.

"Legacy by Mail, Inc." P.O. Box 794, Kula, HI 96790. Phone: 888-876-9364. www.Legacy-By-Mail.com

WEB SITES FOR CLICKER TRAINING

Gail Fisher: www.alldogsgym.com
Karen Pryor: www.karenpryor.com
Gary Wilkes: www.clickandtreat.com

ABOUT THE AUTHORS

Clarice Rutherford is co-author of *Retriever Puppy Training.* A Labrador breeder for more than sixteen years, she is a member of breed and obedience clubs and has competed in breed, obedience, and field events. Mrs. Rutherford obtained a B.S. degree in Animal Science and an M.S. in English from Colorado State University and was employed for several years at the CSU Animal Care Center. She currently is working on two children's books and is training dogs and their owners to participate in animal-assisted activities and animal-assisted therapy.

Through her work in obedience classes, she states she has seen too many dogs living lives of quiet desperation (or, more likely, noisy and hyperactive desperation) — very little stimulation in their environment and lack of consistency in the way their owners treat them. This results from little appreciation for what the dog has to offer us. The dog is a victim of abuse because of the ignorance of people. We have domesticated the dog to the extent that he is totally dependent on humans — and then we abuse him by refusing to understand his needs in the sophisticated world of the twenty-first century. Her goal is to help people understand the nature of the dog they live with, to respect its dogness, and, in return, to be respected by their dog.

David Neil has been a professor in the Faculty of Medicine at the University of Alberta since 1986 and is also the University veterinarian. This follows a decade as Director of Animal Care at Colorado State University, where he and Clarice Rutherford worked together closely on many projects, this book being one of them.

Dr. Neil received his veterinary degree from the University of Liverpool in the United Kingdom in 1959 and was in mixed private practice in Wales and then England for three years. During that time, he came to rely heavily on the almost uncanny ability of the working sheepdogs, particularly where the treatment of large flocks was involved. Throughout his career, many ethical questions have brought him face to face with man's use of, and interactions with, domestic animals. He has been an active participant in the humane movement and was president of the Humane Society for Larimer County (Colorado) from 1978 to 1981. Currently, he is involved with the Canadian Federation of Humane Societies and the Alberta SPCA.

Since the first edition of the puppy book was published in 1981, there has continued to be a great deal of activity in attempting to reduce the large number of unwanted dogs that regrettably must be euthanized each year. The authors remain committed to help deal with this problem by doing what they can to ensure that people end up with a dog they can live with and share much happiness together.

INDEX

leadership concept, 92-98
    dominant family member, 94
    dominant leader, 95
    dominant dog, 98
leash
    for communication, 124
    training, 67, 126-128
    type of, 67
    walking on, 152-153
leg lifting, 159

mounting, 159
mouthiness, 114

neurons, 62-63
neutering, 159-161
night, puppy's first in new home, 48

older dogs and puppies, 8, 59

pack, 12
pack leadership, 103
personality,
    characteristics of different
        types, 100-104
    dependent, 100
    dominant, 103
    eager-to-please, 101-102
    excitable, 103-104
    independent, 100
    shy, 102
    the trainer's, 105
"place," 131-132
play, importance of, 56-59
pretraining activities, 66-71, 74
punishment, 79
puppy mills, 14
puppy temperament testing,
    169-175
    come, 169-170
    energy level, 175
    following, 170
    forgiveness, 172
    elevation dominance, 173
    restraint, 171

retrieving, 173
sight sensitivity, 175
sound sensitivity, 173-175
touch sensitivity, 173

reward, primary and secondary, 126

scruff shaking, 82
self confidence, building of, 73
selecting a puppy, what to look for,
    1-7
separation distress (anxiety), 109,
    155
sexual maturity, 157-158
sexual play, 24
shake can, for discipline, 80, 112
shy puppy, 102
socialization, 18-30, 61, 64-65
spaying, 159-161
squirt bottle, 85-86
stress, exposure to, 34-38
subordinate behavior, 27

teaching puppies, basic information,
    71-74
    be brief, 73
    build confidence, 73
    don't get tough, 73
    keep it simple, 73
    use words, 73
teething, 92, 111
territoriality, 154-155
tethering, 78-79
tidbits, use of, 125
time-out as a discipline, 84-85
toys, 43, 57
training,
    expectations, 138
    equipment, 126
    rewards, use of tidbits, 125

veterinary checkup, 50-51
vinegar water as a discipline, 86
voice, tone of, 79

walk alongside, 128

For a Catalog of Alpine titles
write to:
Alpine Publications, Inc.
P. O. Box 7027
Loveland, CO 80537
or call 1-800-777-7257
check out our website: www.alpinepub.com

ADDITIONAL TITLES OF INTEREST

BETTER BEHAVIOR IN DOGS
William Campbell
Learn more about dog behavior and how you can shape your
dog into your ideal companion. You'll find out how dogs communicate and why you need to be consistent with them at all
times. Learn to correct problem behavior, too.
Softcover   ISBN 1-57779-018-9

THE MENTALLY SOUND DOG
Gail I. Clark and William Boyer
Another viewpoint on dog behavior. You'll find this one especially applicable for larger or difficult-to-control dogs. If you're
really into learning why dogs do what they do and how you can
handle them better, read both books and choose the methods
that work best for your situation.
Softcover   ISBN 0-931866-67-7

PROTECTION DOGS FOR YOU AND YOUR FAMILY
Edward Weiss and Tom Rose
Have a guard dog breed? Want him to be safe with your children
and a good family pet? Then get this book by a noted protection
dog trainer.
Hardcover   ISBN 0-87714-151-7